Letter Crafts

35 CREATIVE PROJECTS FOR STYLISH HOME DECORATIONS

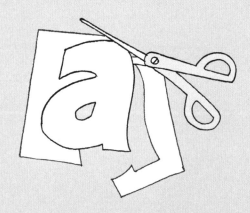

CLARE YOUNGS

CICO BOOKS
LONDON NEW YORK

This edition published in 2018 by CICO Books
an imprint of Ryland Peters & Small Ltd
20–21 Jockey's Fields, London WC1R 4BW
341 E 116th St, New York, NY 10029

www.rylandpeters.com

10 9 8 7 6 5 4 3 2 1

First published in 2014 by CICO Books as
Letter Art

Text © Clare Youngs 2014
Design and photography © CICO Books 2014

A CIP catalog record for this book is available from
the Library of Congress and the British Library.

ISBN: 978-1-78249-600-7

Printed in China

Editor: Anna Southgate
Designers: Carole Ash and Geoff Borin
Photographer: Claire Richardson
Stylist: Clare Youngs
Illustration: Clare and Ian Youngs

Letter Crafts

CONTENTS

Introduction **6**

Getting started **8**

PAPERCRAFT LETTERS **12**

Vintage graphic letters **14**

Wire and paper lettere **18**

Colorful paper bead letters **22**

Sculptural scrollwork **26**

Foamboard lollipop letters **30**

Silver leaf letter **34**

Mexican paper letters **36**

Tissue paper overlay **39**

3-D comic capitals **42**

Notebook cutouts **44**

Simple punched lampshade **46**

Alphabet garland **48**

PAINTED AND PRINTED LETTERS **50**

Painted and printed wood **52**

Ampersand shopper **56**

Painted 3-D outline **60**

Letter-shaped blackboard **63**

Personalized pebbles **66**

Fairground flair **68**

Printed letter art **72**

MIXED-MEDIA LETTERS **76**

Weathered wood letter **78**

Fruit-crate letter **80**

Corrugated capital **82**

String letters **86**

Slot-together letters **88**

Coffee sack letters **92**

Concrete capital **94**

Light it up **96**

Nailed outline **100**

Industrial-style cutouts **102**

Wire cage letter **104**

FABRIC LETTERS **106**

Vintage fabric letter **108**

Mix-it-up fabric magnets **111**

Appliqué wall hanging **114**

Photo transfer **118**

Studded jacket **121**

Templates **124**

Suppliers **141**

Index **142**

Acknowledgments **144**

INTRODUCTION

Letters are an enormous part of our everyday life, to the extent that we can sometimes take them for granted. We are surrounded by letters, on store signs, advertising hoardings, film credits, and even graffiti on the streets. Some letters, like the giant Hollywood in the hills of Los Angeles, have become an iconic symbol that is recognized the word over. From the earliest decorative illuminated manuscripts of the 16th century to the lit-up panels of neon lettering in a restaurant window, to the graphics on a bag from a favorite designer store, they continue to inform, delight, and inspire us.

I learnt the craft of typography as a student of graphic design, and it was during that time that I started to think about the beauty of letterforms, and how you needed both skill and a designer's eye to arrange letters and words so that they were both readable and pleasing to look at. Exploring the different styles of typefaces, I had clear favorites that remain so today. Now, the digital age has opened up the world of typography and letterforms to everyone.

Working with typography has not always been simple. My first job was as a packaging designer. I remember cursing as I tried to fit all the nutritional information, ingredients, product title, and description onto a label the size of a small matchbox! But mainly, what has remained with me, is a love of letters.

As a student, I tried using a letterpress for the first time, playing with the old metal letters, and hand printing on the ancient, heavy, metal printing-presses. I loved the smell of the ink, the feel of the metal letters mounted on wood blocks and the satisfaction of seeing the design come out, freshly printed. I started collecting old printing block letters. I bought them to print from, but also I wanted them purely for the objects themselves. Grouped together, a mixture of tall, small, chunky, and elegant letters made a wonderful display. I then saw some worn, but beautiful gold letters from an old store sign, bought those too, and before I knew it I had started a collection.

In recent years letters have become really popular as an interior design feature. It is easy to see why; displayed singly or in groups, they can add vintage charm or stylish, industrial chic to a room. Creating a look for your home is all about reflecting your personality. You choose to surround yourselves with objects and possessions that are meaningful to you. Whether it is a huge, lit-up statement piece in your living room or a garland of bright, paper letters in your child's room, use letters to reflect your style and creativity. I hope you have as much fun making these projects as I did.

Clare Youngs

GETTING STARTED

FINDING SUITABLE LETTERS

There are literally thousands of typefaces in all shapes and styles. From elegant scripts, classical fonts with serifs, block letters with slab serifs, simple and stylish fonts without serifs, to ornately decorated and novelty alphabets, you are sure to find your own favorites. I have not stated the actual fonts I have used, as it is all down to personal choice. However, when looking for a suitable letter for a project, look at the weight of the typeface I have chosen and try and find one that is similar, or you can simply use one of the templates at the back of the book. It might be that the style and thickness of a particular letter work best for that specific project.

You can find many suitable typefaces on your computer. Enlarge your letter to the right size and print it out. You can then cut this out and use it as a template, or you can use it to trace out and transfer onto your paper or card stock (card). If you need the letter enlarged to a larger size than letter size (A4), the easiest way to do this is using a photocopier.

You can also find great letters in magazines and newspapers. Choose letters that are as big as you can find, and then enlarge them further on a photocopier, if you need to.

ENLARGING TEMPLATES

Some of the templates on pages 124–140 will need to be enlarged. Each template is clearly marked at the percentage of actual size that it is printed, so you will need to enlarge it to the size it is to be used at. For example, if a template is marked as being 25% of actual size, this means that it is a quarter of its actual size and will need to be increased by 400% (four times its size). To do this, enlarge by 200% on a photocopier, and then enlarge that photocopy by another 200%. If a template is 50% of actual size, then it is half of its actual size and will need to be enlarged by 200%. Some projects will need the letter to be bigger than tabloid size (A3). For these, the templates will have to be enlarged in sections and then joined together with tape.

ENLARGING TEMPLATES USING THE GRID METHOD

For large letters, you can use the grid method for enlarging. This is an ideal method if you are making the Letter-shaped Blackboard project on page 63, or the Painted and Printed Wood Letter on page 52 as you have to draw out your letter onto some laminated film (sticky-backed plastic) that has a grid printed onto the backing paper.

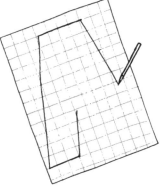

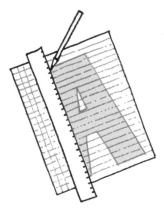

1 Photocopy or trace your template—at the size it appears at the back of this book—onto a letter size (A4) sheet of paper.

2 Mark points at ¾ in. (2 cm) intervals along the top and bottom of the sheet. Join the top and bottom points together using a pencil and ruler. Do the same on the two sides of the paper, joining the marks to make horizontal lines and forming the grid.

3 On a large sheet of paper or tracing paper, do the same but this time make the marks with 1½ in. (4 cm) gaps. This will give you a letter that is twice the size of your original template (200%). You can increase the size of the letter even more by making these squares bigger, for example, to increase it by 400%, draw your grid lines at 3 in. (8 cm) intervals. Now you have to copy the section of the smaller letter scaled up into the larger square.

ADHESIVES

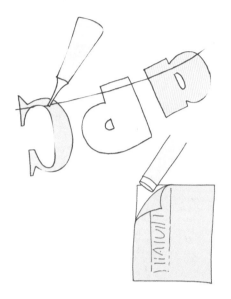

I use different types of glue for different projects, as well as a selection of adhesive tapes. When using glue sticks, try to find one with clear glue because this type never seems to clog up. Wood (PVA) glue is white when it goes on but dries clear and is a very good adhesive for large areas. Use a brush or a small piece of card stock (card) to apply it. Strong, quick-drying glue is clear and usually comes in a tube. You will also need several types of adhesive tape, for instance: masking tape, double-sided tape, and clear tape.

TRACING

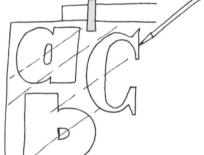

For many projects you need to transfer the template onto paper or card stock (card), using tracing paper. Place a sheet of tracing paper over the template and secure with some masking tape. Trace the lines with a hard 4 (2H) pencil, then turn the tracing paper over and go over the lines again on the reverse with a softer pencil, such as a 2 (HB). Now turn the tracing paper over again and place it in position on your chosen paper or card stock (card). Go over all the lines carefully with the 4 (2H) pencil, and then remove the tracing paper. This will give you a nice, clear outline.

CUTTING

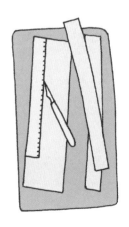

I use a scalpel or craft knife for nearly all my projects. Make sure the blade is sharp and that you always use a cutting mat. When you need to make a straight cut, use a metal ruler and keep the blade in contact with the ruler at all times. Cut toward you, maintaining an even pressure.

SCORING

It is important to score your paper or card stock (card) before making any fold. If it helps, you can draw a pencil line first to help you score in the right place. Place a metal ruler along the line and then score down the line, using the back (blunt) edge of a craft knife or the blunt side of a cutlery knife. Make sure you keep the side of the blade in contact with the ruler.

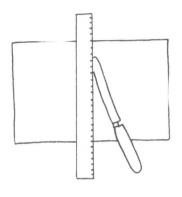

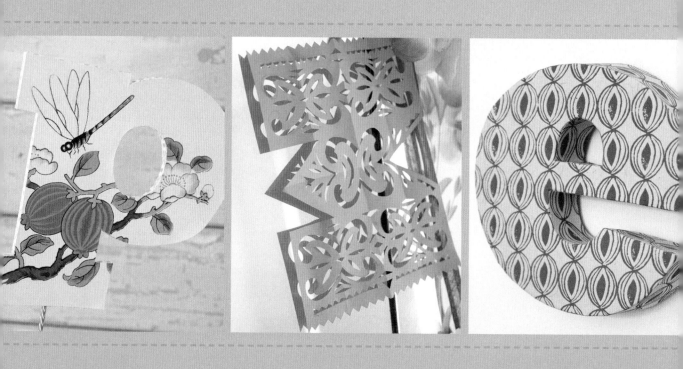

1

Papercraft
LETTERS

VINTAGE GRAPHIC LETTERS

This is a great project for adapting and making covered card stock (card) letters of your own. Once you have mastered the basic method you can make any letter you like and decorate it as you wish. I have covered mine in some gorgeous vintage-style paper, but you could easily use wallpaper to complement the color scheme of a room in your house. Or personalize a letter for a gift, using photographs and written notes.

YOU WILL NEED:

- Letter template
- Plain or graph paper
- Ruler
- Pencil
- Tracing paper
- Masking tape
- Thin card stock (card)
- Craft knife
- Cutting mat
- Patterned paper
- Craft glue

1 Print out your chosen letter from a computer or take a letter from the templates (see page 125) and enlarge it to the desired size. You can either use a photocopier or scale the letter up using graph paper (see page 9). Trace out the letter and transfer it onto the thin card stock (card) (see page 10). Place on a cutting mat and use a craft knife to cut out the shape.

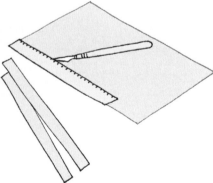

2 Cut strips of card stock (card) for making the sides of your letter: I use the width of my ruler, which is approximately 1½ in. (4 cm). This way you do not have to keep measuring and drawing out the lines.

3 Align a strip of card stock (card) with the edge of your card stock (card) letter, using it to make a right angle. Secure in place using small pieces of masking tape. When you reach a corner, crease the card stock (card) and carry on around the shape.

4 Join another strip of card stock (card) to the first, and then another, until your letter has sides all the way around. You may find it easier to use small strips of card stock (card) at first, joining on each new piece to the last using masking tape.

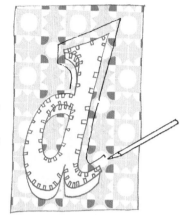

5 Place the patterned paper on your work surface, with the right side facing up. Center the letter shape on the paper, also right side up. Draw around the letter shape, approximately ½ in. (1 cm) away from the edge. Don't worry if it is not exactly ½ in. (1 cm) all the way around—this is simply to give you a glue flap to turn over the edge of the letter. Cut the shape out.

6 Turn the patterned paper shape over, so that it is face down. Spread glue all over the right side of the letter shape and center it, face down, on the back of the patterned paper. Make sure you have an even border of paper all the way around. Press firmly, to make sure it sticks well.

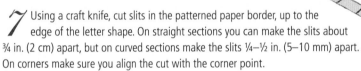

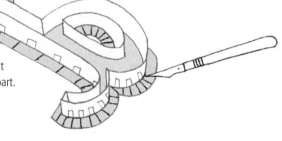

7 Using a craft knife, cut slits in the patterned paper border, up to the edge of the letter shape. On straight sections you can make the slits about ¾ in. (2 cm) apart, but on curved sections make the slits ¼–½ in. (5–10 mm) apart. On corners make sure you align the cut with the corner point.

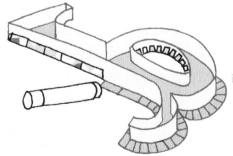

8 Spread glue on the slit paper sections and press them over the edge of the letter shape. You will find it easier to do this a few at a time.

9 To cover the sides of the letter shape, cut strips measuring the same width from the patterned paper and glue in place.

WIRE AND PAPER LETTER

This unusual and delicate letter is made simply by bending some wire into a letter "O" shape and decorating it with strips of paper. I use all sorts of things, from newspaper and magazine pages, to bits of handprinted paper and giftwrap, old labels and wrappers. You can use anything you like. Really mix it up!

YOU WILL NEED:

- Wire
- Tape measure
- Wire cutters
- Masking tape
- Patterned paper
- Craft glue

1 To make the "O" cut two lengths of wire, one measuring 47 in. (120 cm) and the other 32¼ in. (82 cm). Take the longer length and bend it round into a circle, overlapping the ends by about 2 in. (5 cm). Wind a few small pieces of masking tape around the overlap to secure.

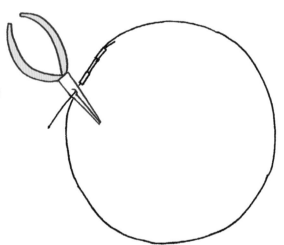

Tip

When shaping the inner section, make sure the overlap is positioned along one of the straight sides so that it is easier to hide the masking tape under paper.

2 Bend the second length of wire into a long sausage shape with straight sides and rounded ends. It needs to fit within the outer circle so that the rounded ends touch it top and bottom. Secure the overlap using small pieces of masking tape.

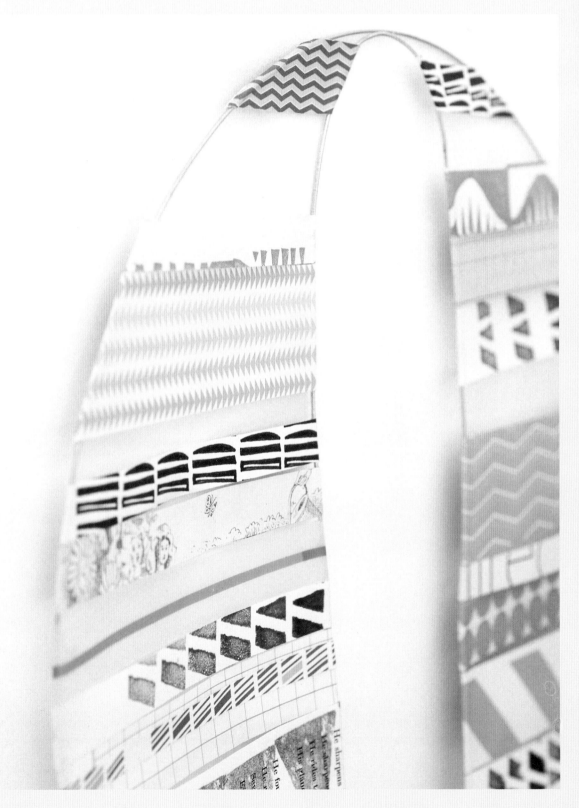

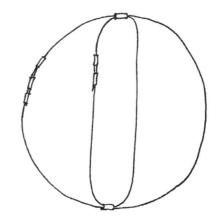

3 Secure the inner section to the outer section at the top and bottom, using masking tape. When doing this, position the overlapped section of the outer circle to one of the sides so that you can hide it under some paper strips.

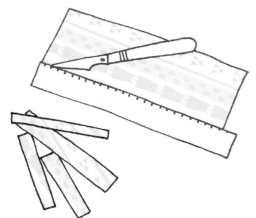

4 Protecting your work surface with a cutting mat, cut strips of paper of varying lengths (mine were between 3½ and 8½ in. (9 and 16 cm). The end result will be more interesting if you vary the widths, too.

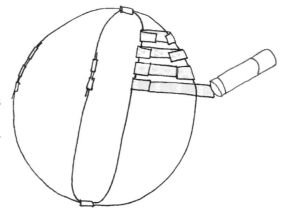

5 Working with the letter shape face down on your surface, thread a strip of paper behind the inner and outer sections of wire on one side of the letter. Dot glue on each end and fold these over the wire, sticking them to the back of the paper strip.

6 To keep it all looking neat, trim off any little corners or edges that do not align properly. Often the back of the letter is just as interesting as the front. I like to leave some gaps so that you can see that the letter is made from wire.

7 Once you have completed your design, either remove the small bits of masking tape holding the two wire sections together, or stick a piece of patterned paper over each of them.

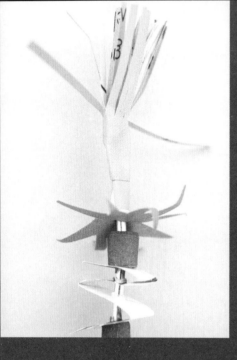

COLORFUL PAPER BEAD LETTERS

Use strips of colorful paper to make pretty beads or to fashion mini flags and tassels. Cut little paper stars and flowers and thread all of your shapes onto some wire to create these unusual letters.

1 These instructions are for making a lower case "a." To make the "b" and "c" you will find it helpful to draw a simple outline of each letter, at the size of you want it to be, to act as a guide when it comes to bending the wire.

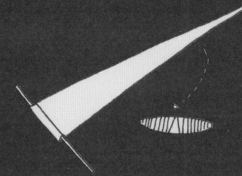

2 Make a collection of beads in different shapes and sizes. To make a basic paper bead, cut a strip of paper measuring 4 x ½ in. (10 x 1 cm). Spread glue along one short end of the strip. Using a spare piece of wire, wrap the glued end of the paper strip around the wire, and roll the rest of the paper up tightly to form the bead. About halfway through rolling the bead, you can pull it from the wire to prevent the paper sticking permanently.

3 Vary the width of the strip of paper to give you different-sized beads. To make a tapered bead of a different shape, cut a long triangle from the paper and roll in the same way, starting from the base of the triangle and working up to the point.

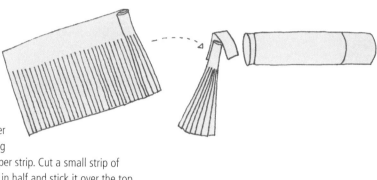

4 To make a tassel, cut a strip of paper measuring 3 x 1½ in. (8 x 4 cm). Make a fringe along the bottom long edge of the paper, cutting every ⅛ in. (2 mm), and leaving ½ in. (1 cm) uncut along the top edge of the paper. Roll the strip of paper in exactly the same way as you would a bead, dabbing some glue in one of the top (uncut) corners of the paper strip. Cut a small strip of paper approximately ¼ x ¾ in. (5 mm x 2 cm). Fold it in half and stick it over the top of the tassel leaving a ⅛ in. (2 mm) gap at the top for threading onto the wire.

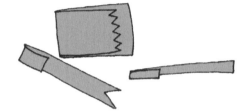

5 Cut small flags in different shapes. Fold over one short edge of each flag (either a little way or halfway) and glue the fold in place, leaving enough room to thread the flag onto the wire.

6 You can also, cut small flower shapes, triangles, stars, and leaf shapes ready for threading. Fold strips of paper up, concertina-style, to add to the collection.

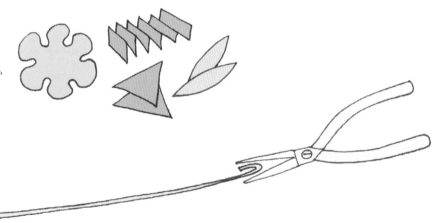

7 Cut a length of wire approximately 13½ in. (34 cm) in length. Use pliers to make a small loop at one end of the wire. This will stop the beads falling off as you thread them.

8 Thread the beads and shapes onto the wire. Use an awl or similar sharp implement to make holes in any shapes that need them.

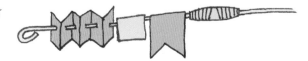

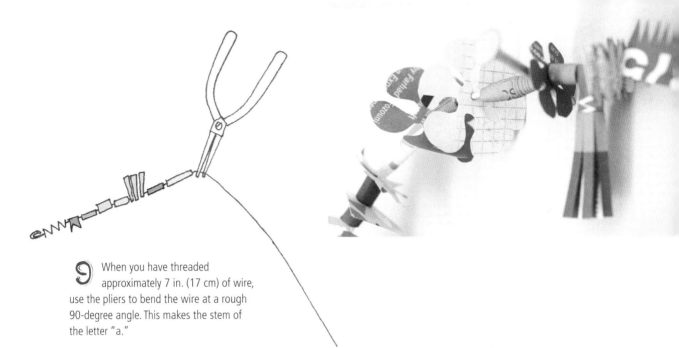

9 When you have threaded approximately 7 in. (17 cm) of wire, use the pliers to bend the wire at a rough 90-degree angle. This makes the stem of the letter "a."

10 Carry on threading the shapes, until you are ½ in. (1 cm) from the end. Now bend the wire to make the bowl of the letter "a." Use pliers to loop the working end of the wire around the stem, to secure the joint. Make this loop roughly 2¾ in. (7 cm) up from the bottom of the stem, nestled between two paper shapes.

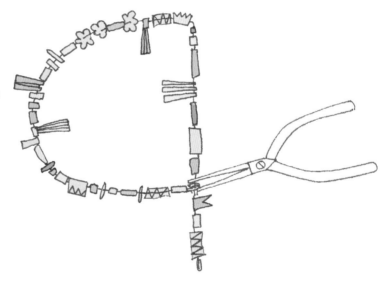

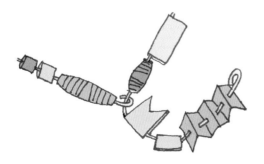

11 Make a curve in the 2¾ in. (7 cm) section of the straight edge, to form the tail of the letter "a."

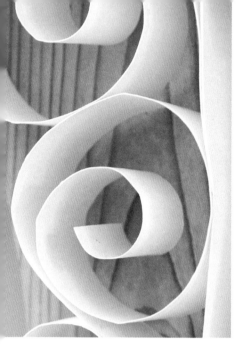

SCULPTURAL SCROLLWORK

Using just a few strips of plain white paper, you can create beautifully elegant and ornate letters. You could use this technique to make a lovely gift for a special friend. Making curled scrolls is very simple, but make sure you hang it quite high—choose a place where it can make a big impact—as your finished letter will be quite fragile.

1 Choose your letter and enlarge it to the right size, either by using a photocopier or by scaling the letter up on graph paper (see page 9). Choose a simple typeface—it is important that the main shape is easy to construct, leaving the paper scrollwork to create the decorative element. My letter measured approximately 10 in. (25 cm) in height. Transfer the letter onto some tracing paper (see page 10).

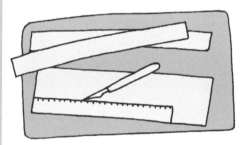

2 Protecting your work surface with a cutting mat, use a craft knife to cut some strips of thick cartridge paper. Use the width of your ruler, so that you can cut the strips without having to measure and mark each time. My ruler measured 1¼ in. (3 cm) across.

3 Construct a basic structure for your letter. Place your traced letter on a flat surface and use this as a guide. Align one of the cartridge paper strips with the outline of the letter, but at right angles to it. Follow the shape of the letter and when you get to a change of direction, fold the strip and carry on.

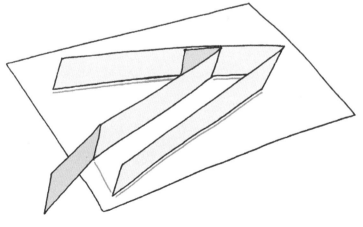

4 When you come to the end of one strip, overlap a new strip by approximately ¾ in. (2 cm) and glue the two strips together. When you reach the end of the outline, overlap the final strip by ¾ in. (2 cm) and glue to join. It may be difficult to keep your letter in shape, but this is not a problem. Once you start to add the paper curls, the letter will hold its shape better.

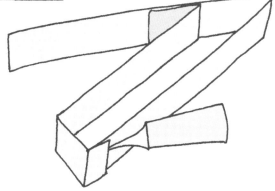

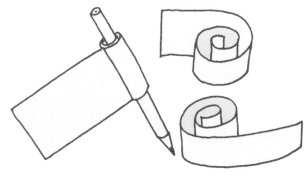

5 Cut more strips from the cartridge paper. Vary the lengths, from 6 to 20 in. (15 to 50 cm). Take one of the strips and curl one end around a pencil. Wind the paper around the pencil tightly, leaving a short length uncurled at the end. Repeat with the other strips.

6 Arrange several scrolls within the main structure of the letter. You want to fill the space with different sized scrolls. Starting at the bottom of the letter, use the scrolls to secure areas of the letter that could pull out of place. Glue at points where the scrolls touch the sides of the letter and butt up against each other.

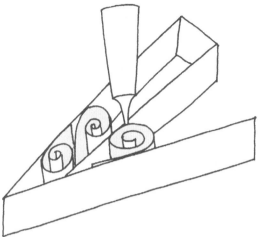

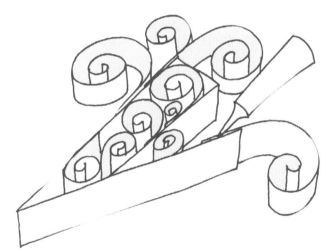

7 Now glue some larger, looser scrolls to the outside of the letter, so that they extend over the top of the shape and out to the side. It is a good idea to experiment with different sized scrolls before you stick anything down.

8 If your letter has a "floating" inner part, like the bowl of a letter "P," make the bowl outline in the same way as you made the outer shape. The outer section of the letter won't take its proper form until you insert the inner section and use the scrolls to pull it into shape.

FOAMBOARD LOLLIPOP LETTERS

Use colorful scraps of wallpaper and pages from old books to create a collection of letters with a lovely vintage appeal. The thin sticks are available from craft stores. Cut them to different lengths to make a charming display for a shelf in a child's bedroom.

1 Choose your letter from the templates on page 136 and enlarge it to the right size, either by using a photocopier or scaling the letter up on graph paper (see page 9). I made mine approximately 8 in. (20 cm) in height. Trace out the letter and transfer it onto a piece of foamboard (see page 10). Protecting your work surface with a cutting mat, cut out the shape using a craft knife and a ruler for any straight edges.

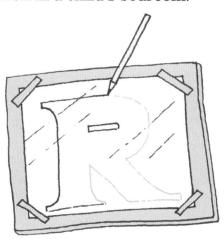

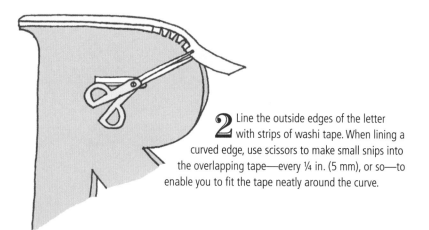

2 Line the outside edges of the letter with strips of washi tape. When lining a curved edge, use scissors to make small snips into the overlapping tape—every ¼ in. (5 mm), or so—to enable you to fit the tape neatly around the curve.

3 Spread glue all over the front of the letter shape and place a piece of patterned paper, right side up, over the top. Smooth out and press down all over. Allow the glue to dry before using a craft knife to cut off any overlapping paper. You'll find this easier to do if you place your letter face down on your cutting mat. Repeat on the other side of the letter, using a different paper if you like, so that both sides are covered.

4 Cut a length of stick. Cut a strip of washi tape to the same length and lay it down on your work surface, sticky side up. Place the stick on the tape and wrap the tape around the stick neatly, to cover it.

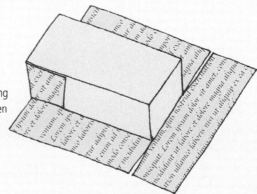

5 To cover the block of wood, center it on a page taken from an old book. Draw around the base. Remove the block and draw a border around your drawn outline. It needs to be the same depth as the sides of the block. Use a pencil and a ruler to mark cutting guides as shown. Cut along these guides to make four flaps.

6 Spread glue all over the wrong side of the paper and place the block back in position. Wrap the two short sides of the block first, sticking the paper flaps to the long sides of the block. Then wrap the two long sides.

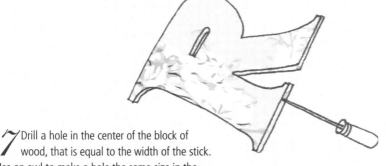

7 Drill a hole in the center of the block of wood, that is equal to the width of the stick. Use an awl to make a hole the same size in the foamboard at the base of the letter.

8 Push the stick into the wooden base and then push the letter onto the opposite end of the stick.

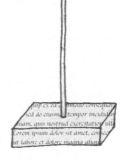

SILVER LEAF LETTER

If you have already tried the Vintage Graphic Letters on pages 14–17, you will find this easy to make. The method for making the letter is the same, but this time the sides of the letter create a rim within which to decorate the front of the letter. I have used some silver leaf and vibrant, dark-orange card for a stunning, contemporary look.

YOU WILL NEED:

- Letter template
- Plain or graph paper
- Ruler
- Pencil
- Tracing paper
- Masking tape
- Thick card stock (card) measuring 22 x 20 in. (56 x 50 cm)
- Craft knife
- Cutting mat
- Spray adhesive
- Face mask
- Silver leaf (I find the type on backing paper the easiest to use)
- Kitchen scourer
- Thin white card stock (card)
- Craft glue
- Thin card stock (card) or thick paper in a strong color

1 Print out your chosen letter from a computer or take a letter from the templates (see page 124) and enlarge it to the desired size. You can either use a photocopier or scale the letter up using graph paper (see page 9). Trace out the letter and transfer it onto the thick card stock (card) (see page 10). Protecting your work surface with a cutting mat, use a craft knife to cut out the shape.

2 Lightly spray a section of the letter with adhesive. You should always wear a mask and follow the instructions for use. Place a sheet of silver leaf face down on the sprayed area, rub down, and then remove the backing sheet. Don't worry too much if there are a few bits that haven't gone down well. This all adds to the distressed finish. Repeat the process until you have applied silver leaf all over the front of the letter.

3 Once the letter is covered, rub over parts of the surface with a new kitchen scourer to give an interesting, distressed finish.

4 Follow steps 2 to 4 from the Vintage Graphic letters on pages 14–17 to make the sides of the letter. Make sure all the masking tape is on the outside of the letter and when you add a new strip of card stock (card), butt the two edges together as neatly as you can.

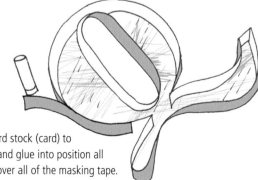

5 Cut some strips of colored paper or thin card stock (card) to the same width as the sides of your letter, and glue into position all around the outer edge of the letter. Be sure to cover all of the masking tape.

MEXICAN PAPER LETTERS

In Mexico, during celebrations and festivals, colorful garlands and flags cut from tissue paper adorn the houses and streets. Make your own paper bunting and turn a birthday party into a real fiesta, Mexican style! The instructions here are for a letter that includes a curved section and a straight section. From this you should be able to make any letter of the alphabet.

YOU WILL NEED:

- Letter templates
- Plain or graph paper
- Ruler
- Pencil
- Tracing paper
- Masking tape
- Thin colored paper
- Small, pointed paper-cutting scissors
- Craft knife
- Cutting mat
- Craft glue
- Ribbon or tape

1 Choose your first letter, or use the template on page 126, and enlarge it to the right size, either by using a photocopier or scaling the letter up on graph paper (see page xx). I made mine approximately 6 in. (15 cm) tall. Trace out the letter, transfer the trace onto a thin piece of colored paper (see page 10), and use scissors to cut it out.

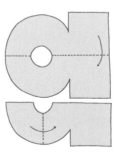

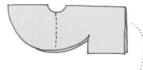

2 Follow the illustration on the left to fold the bowl of the letter into four. You are in fact folding the whole letter, but you will work on this circular section first.

Tips for cutting

Take care when positioning your shapes, as you might lose an entire section of a letter shape if you cut across a fold in the wrong place. It is okay to cut into the shape from any edge, but do not cut all the way across.

Once you have worked on one section and refolded the shape to work on another section, make sure you avoid cutting into any patterns already made.

3 On the illustration on the left is a guide to some shapes that you can cut out. You can follow these or you can make up your own. These letters are easy to make, so have a little practice and experiment with your shapes. As with cutting paper snowflakes at Christmas, it is always a lovely surprise when you open the shape out and see the pattern you have made.

4 When you have finished cutting the circular section, unfold the letter and refold it, following the illustrations on the right, to concentrate on the stem of the letter.

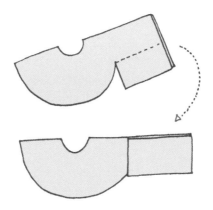

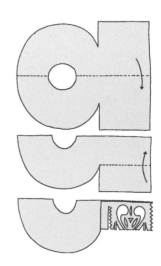

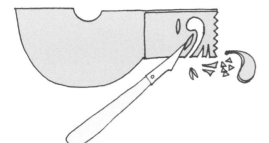

5 Cut out some shapes. On this section you will see on the illustration to the left that a few of the shapes are cut from the middle, rather than from one of the edges. You will need to use a craft knife for cutting these.

6 When you have made as many letters as you need, place a small blob of glue at the top of each one and attach it to a length of ribbon or tape.

TISSUE PAPER OVERLAY

I love using tissue paper in craft projects, especially when overlapping layers to create different shades and areas of color. Using three or four cut-out shapes, you can create wonderfully abstract designs. Add contrast by choosing different typefaces and group several letters together for an eye-catching display with a contemporary look.

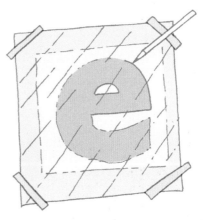

YOU WILL NEED:

- Letter templates
- Plain or graph paper
- Ruler
- Pencil
- Tracing paper
- Masking tape
- Scissors
- Sheets of tissue paper in different colors
- White cartridge paper
- Spray adhesive
- Face mask
- Eraser

1 Choose your letters from any of the templates at the back of the book and enlarge them to the right size, either by using a photocopier or by scaling the letters up on graph paper (see page 9). I made mine approximately 6 in. (15 cm) in height. Lay some tissue paper over the first of your chosen letters, secure with masking tape, and trace out the outline.

2 Cut out the letter. Repeat with more letters in different typefaces and contrasting widths. Use a different colored tissue paper each time.

3 Play with the letters on a piece of white cartridge paper. Move them around, trying different combinations of overlays and positions, until you have an arrangement that you like. Mark lightly around some of the letter edges using a pencil, in order to remember the position of each one, then remove each layer until you reach the letter at the bottom.

4 Coat the back of the first letter with a light layer of spray adhesive. Be sure to follow the manufacturer's instructions and wear a face mask. Place the letter on the cartridge paper and smooth down. Repeat, to stick down each letter in turn. Gently remove any pencil marks you may have made using an eraser.

Tip

When it comes to Step 3, there are various ways to remember the design and sequence of sticking. Instead of marking some of the letter edges, you could either draw a little sketch of the design or take a digital photo of it.

3-D COMIC CAPITALS

This method of making letters is so easy. The flat posterboard (cardboard) shapes are mounted on blocks for a great 3-D effect. I have used old comics—ideal for a child's bedroom. Rescue worn-out books from the recycling bin and give some of the pages a new lease on life.

YOU WILL NEED:

- Pages from old comics or books
- Thick posterboard (cardboard)
- Glue stick
- Letter template
- Plain or graph paper
- Ruler
- Pencil
- Tracing paper
- Masking tape
- Craft knife
- Cutting mat
- Mounting board in different colors
- Craft glue
- Old plastic cotton spools

1 Glue the comic page onto the posterboard (cardboard).

2 Choose your letter, or use the templates on page 127, and enlarge it to the right size, either by using a photocopier or scaling the letter up on graph paper (see page 9). I made mine approximately 12 in. (30 cm) in height and used a condensed typeface in order to make the letter as big as possible for the size of comic I was using.

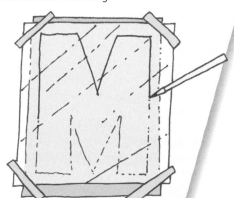

3 Trace out the letter and transfer it to the back of the posterboard (cardboard) (see page 10), making sure you draw the shape in reverse, so that it faces the right way once you have cut it out and turned the posterboard (cardboard) over.

4 Protecting your work surface with a cutting mat, use a craft knife to cut out the letter.

5 Place the letter face down onto the back of a piece of colored mounting board. Draw around the letter using a sharp pencil. Again, remember to draw the shape in reverse. Cut the shape out and turn the mounting board over.

6 Glue the comic book letter on top of the colored mounting board letter. Position the mounting board slightly off-center, so that it protrudes to the side and below, to form a drop shadow. It is best to do this by eye, as each letter will form a different shadow. On my "M" I moved the colored mounting board approximately ½ in. (1 cm) to the right and lowered it by approximately ¾ in. (2 cm).

7 Stick a couple of old plastic cotton spools to the back of the letter to make the letter stand proud of the wall when you mount it.

NOTEBOOK CUTOUTS

Transform and personalize plain brown notebooks using bold cutouts and sheets of colored paper. Use tape to add a brightly colored spine for an original finishing touch.

1 Choose your letter, or use the templates on page 127, and enlarge it to the right size, either by using a photocopier or scaling the letter up on graph paper (see page 9). The letter needs to fit on the front cover of the notebook, at least ½ in. (1 cm) from the edges of the book all the way around. Trace out the letter and transfer it to the book cover (see page xx).

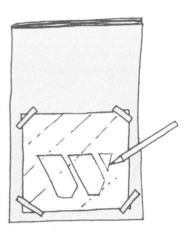

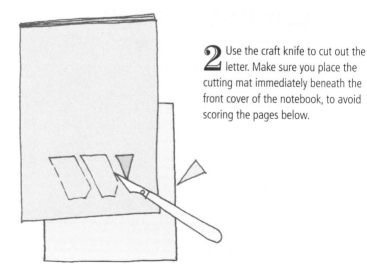

2 Use the craft knife to cut out the letter. Make sure you place the cutting mat immediately beneath the front cover of the notebook, to avoid scoring the pages below.

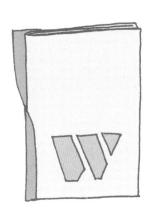

3 Cut a length of fabric tape to match the height of the book. Spread glue on the back of the tape and stick it down the spine of the notebook.

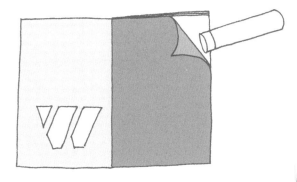

4 Cut a sheet of colored paper to match the size of the pages in the notebook. Glue one side of the paper and stick it to the first page of the book.

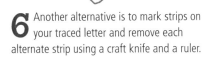

5 Vary your cutout by using a hole punch to make holes evenly around the traced letter outline. Erase any remaining pencil marks once you have finished.

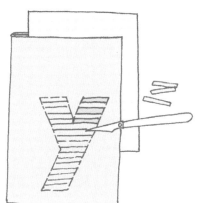

6 Another alternative is to mark strips on your traced letter and remove each alternate strip using a craft knife and a ruler.

SIMPLE PUNCHED LAMPSHADE

The lamp base I used here has three small legs with a ring of metal that allows a paper shade to sit safely away from the bulb. Look on craft websites to find something similar or buy a light from a store and use the shade provided. You can also use the shade in this project with a votive. Make sure you place the votive in a glass jar for safety.

YOU WILL NEED:

- Letter template
- Plain or graph paper
- Ruler
- Pencil
- Tracing paper
- Masking tape
- Craft knife
- Cutting mat
- Thin card stock (card) measuring 23¾ in. long by 10½ in. high (58 x 26 cm)
- Hole punch
- Hammer
- Eraser
- Craft glue

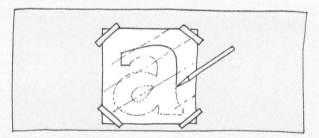

1 Choose your letter, or use the template on page 128, and enlarge it to the right size, either by using a photocopier or scaling the letter up on graph paper (see page xx). I made mine approximately 4 in. (10 cm) in height. Protecting your work surface with a cutting mat, use a craft knife to cut out the shape. Trace out the letter and transfer it onto the strip of card stock (card), positioning it in the center and approximately 2½ in. (6 cm) up from the bottom edge.

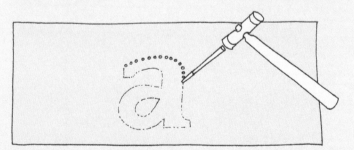

2 Using a hole punch and hammer, make holes evenly around the outline of the letter. Mine have around ⅛ in. (3 mm) between each one. Remember to use a cutting mat to protect your work surface.

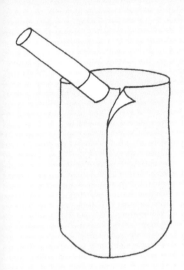

3 Use an eraser to remove any pencil lines. Curl the shade into a cylinder shape, glue along one short edge and stick the two ends together.

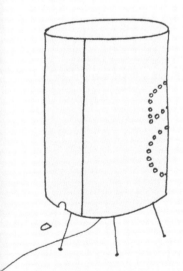

4 If necessary, cut a small semicircle from the bottom edge (toward the rear of the shade) so that the shade fits neatly over the cord of the lamp base.

ALPHABET GARLAND

Brighten up a corner of a child's bedroom with this colorful alphabet. For added contrast, use a different typeface for each letter—some tall and thin, others chunky and condensed. This is an ideal project to use up all those lovely birthday cards you can't bear to throw away. The more colors and patterns you use, the more fun the garland looks!

YOU WILL NEED:

- Letter templates
- Plain or graph paper
- Ruler
- Pencil
- Tracing paper
- Masking tape
- Patterned posterboard (carboard) or patterned paper and thin card stock (card)
- Craft knife
- Cutting mat
- Craft glue
- Colored ribbon or tape

1 Choose your letters, using a different typeface for each one, or use the templates on page 129. Enlarge them to the right size, either by using a photocopier or by scaling the letter up on graph paper (see page 9). I made mine approximately 4–4¾ in. (10–12 cm) in height. Transfer the letters onto some tracing paper (see page 10).

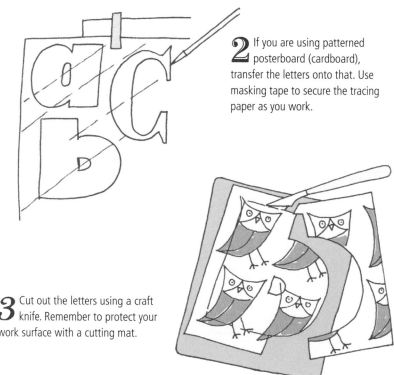

2 If you are using patterned posterboard (cardboard), transfer the letters onto that. Use masking tape to secure the tracing paper as you work.

3 Cut out the letters using a craft knife. Remember to protect your work surface with a cutting mat.

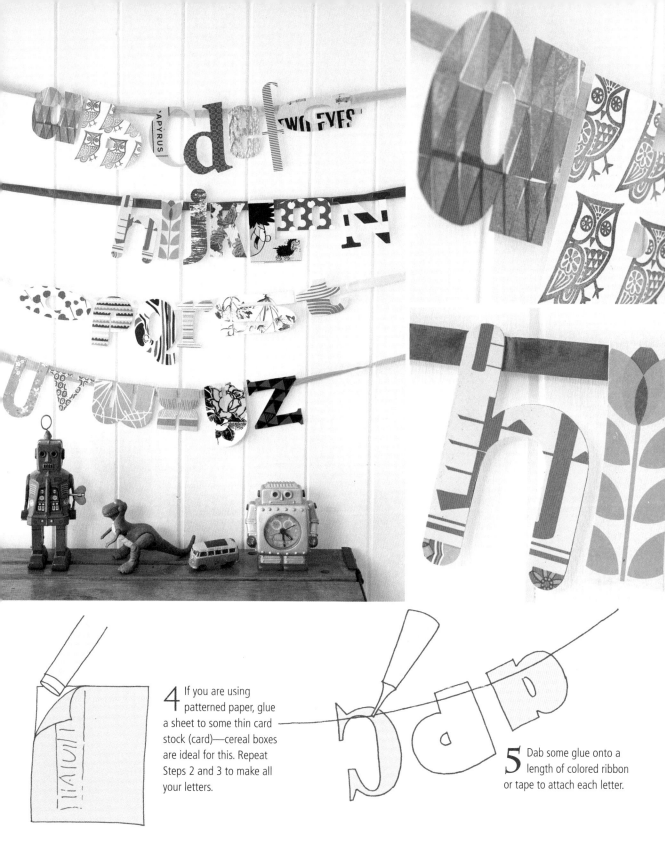

4 If you are using patterned paper, glue a sheet to some thin card stock (card)—cereal boxes are ideal for this. Repeat Steps 2 and 3 to make all your letters.

5 Dab some glue onto a length of colored ribbon or tape to attach each letter.

2

Printed and painted
LETTERS

PAINTED AND PRINTED WOOD

This large letter, painted and printed on a section of wood, makes a real statement piece and provides a stunning addition to a contemporary interior. I have used some lovely, rough-looking wood that started life as a shelf in a tile factory. See if you can find a suitable piece of wood at a salvage yard. Or use a new piece of wood and give it some age by painting it a pale color and sanding it down.

1 Choose your letter or use the template on page 130. Use a craft knife to cut a piece of laminating film (sticky-backed plastic) to the length you need. My letter is 22 in. (56 cm) high and 13½ in. (34 cm) wide. You need at least a 4 in. (10 cm) border all around the letter.

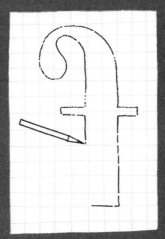

2 Lay the laminating film (sticky-backed plastic) on your work surface, with the film (plastic) facing down and the paper backing facing upward. The backing paper usually has a grid marked on it so that you can enlarge your chosen letter using the grid method (see page 9). You will be flipping the stencil over when it comes to using it, so draw your letter facing the opposite way.

3 Protecting your work surface with a cutting mat, use a craft knife to cut out the shape. Position the stencil on top of your wood, with the backing paper side down.

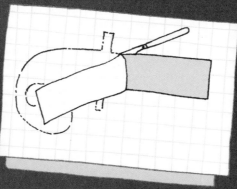

4 Starting in one corner, gently peel the paper back—you'll need to get your hand in underneath the stencil. Work slowly, pressing the film (plastic) flat onto the wood as you go. Make sure it is pressed down firmly.

5 Paint your letter in a color of your choice. When you come to the edge of the stencil use the brush in an upright position and make a gentle stabbing motion to apply the paint. This will stop any paint seeping underneath the stencil.

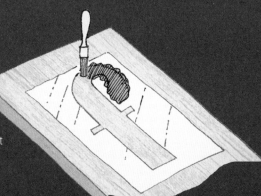

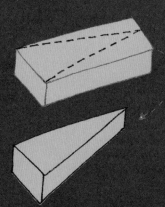

6 Use the craft knife and a ruler to cut a triangle from the eraser and use it as a stamp to print a pattern of triangles in silver ink.

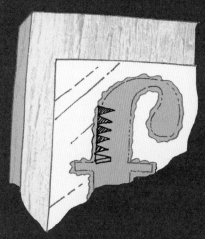

7 As you print, overlap the edges of the stencil slightly so that, when you peel off the film (plastic), there are no gaps at the edges of your letter.

8 Once the paint is dry, peel the film (plastic) stencil away.

AMPERSAND SHOPPER

Stencils are very easy to make and once you have learned the technique you can use the method for all sorts of things. Here, a big and bold ampersand looks great on this useful shopping bag. The project includes instructions for making the bag, too, but you could always buy a readymade canvas bag from a craft supplier. I have used scrim, but any cotton fabric would work well.

YOU WILL NEED:

- Letter template
- Roll of 45 cm (17¾ in.) wide laminating film (sticky-backed plastic)
- Cutting mat
- Craft knife
- Pencil
- Fabric measuring 32 x 17¾ in. (80 x 45 cm)
- Newspaper
- Small pot of paint or fabric dye
- Saucer
- Piece of sponge
- Pins
- Sewing machine
- Length of herringbone tape (webbing) measuring 31½ in. (80 cm)
- Scissors

1 Follow steps 1 and 2 from the Painted and Printed Wood project (page 52) to draw up your stencil from the laminated film (sticky-backed plastic). My ampersand is 10 in. (25 cm) tall (see template on page 130), but you can make yours any size as long as it fits on the front of the finished bag, which measures 11 x 16 in. (28 x 40 cm). Protecting your work surface with a cutting mat, cut the shape out, taking care with the holes in the center.

2 Fold the fabric in half, with wrong sides facing and short edges together. Position your stencil on what will become the front of the bag (with the folded edge of the fabric to the left). You need to allow for a seam ½ in. (1 cm) in from the side and bottom edges, and a 2½ in. (5 cm) hem at the top. I positioned my ampersand 2¼ in. (6 cm) in from the right edge and 4½ in. (11 cm) up from the bottom.

3 Follow step 4 from the Painted and Printed Wood project (page 54) to remove the backing from the film (plastic). Position the film (plastic) for the holes in the center of the shape in the same way. Make sure that the film (plastic) is pressed down firmly all over.

4 Open up the fabric and place some newspaper under the half with the stencil on. Pour some of the fabric dye or paint into a saucer and dab a bit onto the piece of sponge. Apply the dye to the fabric using a dabbing motion and taking extra care at the edges of the stencil. Once the dye is dry, carefully peel off the film (plastic) stencil.

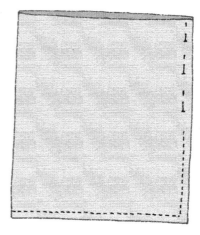

5 Re-fold the fabric—this time, with right sides facing. Pin along the bottom and open side of the bag. Sew a ½ in. (1 cm) seam along these two edges. For strength, stitch a row of zigzag along the raw edges.

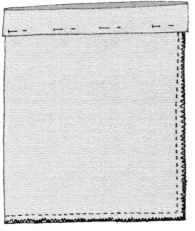

6 Fold over a ½ in. (1 cm) hem along the top of the bag and then fold over an additional 1½ in. (4 cm) hem and pin in position. Sew a line of stitching along this hem.

7 Use scissors to cut the strip of herringbone tape (webbing) in half, so that you have two lengths of 16 in. (40 cm). These are your bag handles. Pin the ends of the first handle on opposite sides of the bag, 3 in. (8 cm) in from the side edge and lining up the bottom of the tape with the hem you sewed in step 6.

8 To attach each end of the handle to the bag, stitch a row of close zigzag along the bottom of the tape, where it aligns with the hem, and a second row along the top of the bag. Stitch a third row between these two lines.

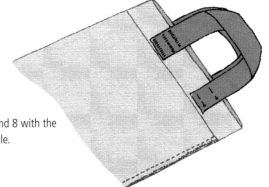

9 Repeat steps 7 and 8 with the second bag handle.

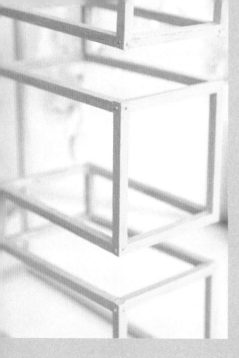

PAINTED 3-D OUTLINE

Large wooden letters make great statement pieces in a contemporary interior. You don't have to get any major tools out for this one—not even a saw—as you can cut this type of wood using a craft knife. You can adapt the design to make other letters of the alphabet but remember you can only use straight lines.

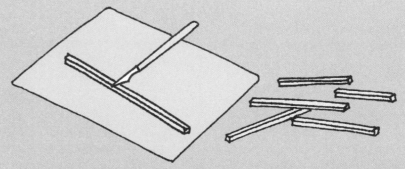

1 Start by cutting lengths of baton to make the front of your letter. For this "E," I used the following lengths of baton: one x 14 in. (35 cm), four x 4¾ in. (12.5 cm), two x 9 in. (22 cm), three x 3¾ in. (9.5 cm), and two x 2 in. (5 cm).

2 Lay the baton lengths out flat on your work surface, in position.

3 Starting at the top left, align the corners of the letter stem and top bar, and push a pin through the two sections of wood to secure. Balsa wood is soft, but you will need a thimble or something similar to help drive the pin home, and to protect your fingers.

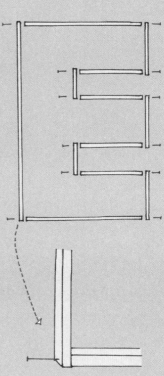

4 Continue to join the remaining lengths of baton together in the same way, until you have made your first letter shape. Make a second, identical, letter shape following the same steps.

5 To achieve the 3-D effect, you need a short baton at each corner of the letter—in this case 12 batons. Mine measured 3 in. (8 cm) in length.

6 Starting at the four outermost corners join the two letter shapes together by securing one of the short batons between two corresponding corners. Continue adding the batons from corner to corner as shown.

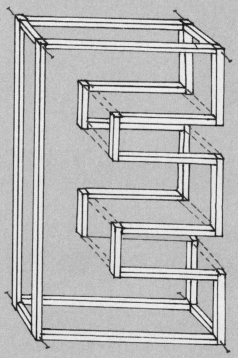

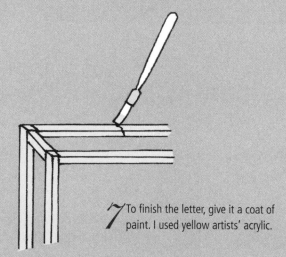

7 To finish the letter, give it a coat of paint. I used yellow artists' acrylic.

LETTER-SHAPED BLACKBOARD

Not only will this "blackboard" letter look stunning in your kitchen, it will prove really useful, too. Whether you use it as a reminder to buy more milk or for a message to make sure the dog gets fed, you will wonder how you ever managed without it!

1 Coat the plywood with a layer of white emulsion paint. If you like, when it is dry you can sand down some sections to give the board a nice weathered look.

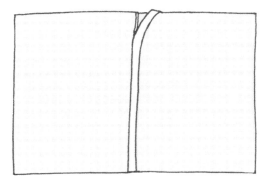

2 Cut two lengths of laminating film (sticky-backed plastic), each measuring 24 in. (60 cm). Lay the two pieces on your work surface, backing paper side up. Align the long edges without overlapping them and join with masking tape.

YOU WILL NEED:

- Plywood measuring 24 x 24 in. (60 x 60 cm)
- White emulsion paint
- Paintbrush
- Sandpaper (optional)
- Roll of 17¾ in. (45 cm) wide laminating film (sticky-backed plastic)
- Pencil
- Masking tape
- Craft knife
- Cutting mat
- Blackboard paint

3 Laminating film (sticky-backed plastic) usually has a grid marked on it. Use this to enlarge your chosen letter using the grid method (see page 9). Mine measured approximately 21½ in. (55 cm) (see the template on page 131). You will be flipping the stencil over when it comes to using it, so draw your letter facing the opposite way. Position the letter so that the inside of the bowl does not overlap the join between the two pieces of film (plastic).

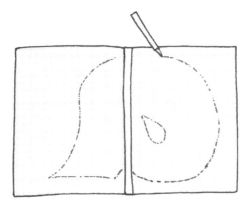

4 Protecting your work surface with a cutting mat, use a craft knife to cut out the letter. Leave the shape for the inside of the bowl to one side while you position the stencil on the plywood base—a second pair of hands would be useful here. Center the letter on the plywood, with the backing paper facing down.

5 Starting in one corner, remove the backing paper. You need to get your hand up underneath the stencil and work slowly, pressing the film (plastic) flat onto the plywood as you go. Make sure it is pressed down well. You can also remove the masking tape as you go.

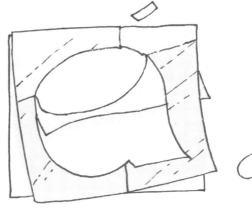

6 Place the inside of the bowl in position and remove the backing paper.

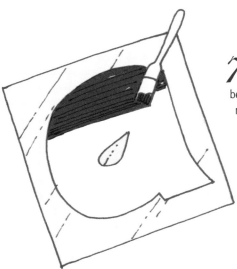

7 Use blackboard paint to fill in the letter, taking extra care at the edges. The laminating film (sticky-backed plastic) should be stuck down well to prevent any paint seeping under. You may need two layers of paint for a good finish.

8 When the paint is dry carefully remove the stencil. If any black paint has seeped under the film (plastic), go over it with a few layers of white paint.

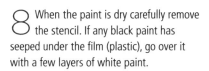

PERSONALIZED PEBBLES

These pebble letters are simple to make and are perfect as a gift for someone special. I like the contrast of white ink on the dark gray, but if your pebbles are pale in color use black ink instead. I used a thin ink pen to draw on fine details—this is your chance to play with decorative patterns on letters.

YOU WILL NEED:

- Pebbles
- Tracing paper
- Pencil
- Scissors
- Masking tape
- White ink pen

1 Trace out a letter of a suitable size for your pebble (see page 10) or use the templates on page 132). Use scissors to cut it out.

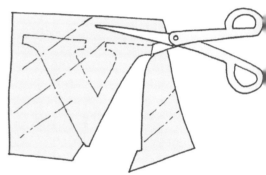

2 Roll a small piece of masking tape into a tube shape and use this to secure the template in position on the pebble. Repeat as many times as necessary to keep the template from slipping.

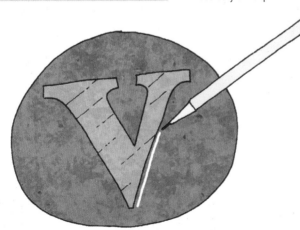

3 Use the white ink pen to draw the outline of the letter shape very carefully onto the pebble.

4 Remove the template. Now you can use the white ink pen to fill in the letter shape with a pattern.

Tip

Don't worry if you make a mistake as you work. You can either wash all the ink off and start again or simply turn the pebble over.

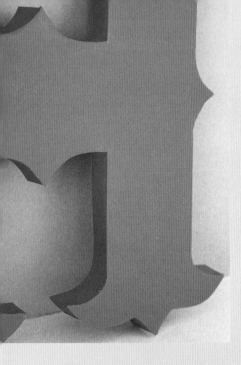

FAIRGROUND FLAIR

There is no shortage of inspiration for creative letter crafts. On posters, storefronts, newspapers, road signs, and bags—interesting shapes and forms are all around us. I am always on the lookout for interesting typography. The inspiration for this gorgeous red letter came from ornate fairground lettering. The letter's shaped edges make it a little trickier to make than other projects, but it is well worth the effort.

YOU WILL NEED:

- Letter template
- Plain or graph paper
- Ruler
- Pencil
- Tracing paper
- Masking tape
- Craft knife
- Cutting mat
- Foamboard measuring approximately 16 x 16 in. (40 x 40 cm)
- Thin, colored card stock (card)
- Scissors
- Craft glue

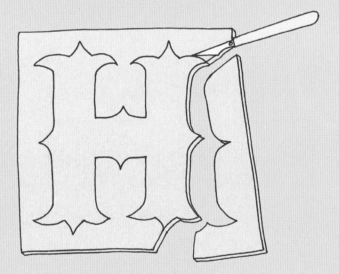

1 Choose your letter, or use the template on page 133, and enlarge it to the right size, either by using a photocopier or scaling the letter up on graph paper (see page xx). I made mine approximately 13½ in. wide by 15 in. tall (34 x 38 cm). Protecting your work surface with a cutting mat, use a craft knife to cut out the shape. Trace out the letter and transfer it onto a piece of foamboard (see page 10). Cut out the shape using a craft knife and a ruler for any straight edges.

2 Cut long strips of thin, colored card stock (card). Use the width of your ruler, so that you can cut the strips without having to measure and mark each time. My ruler measured 1½ in. (3.5 cm) across.

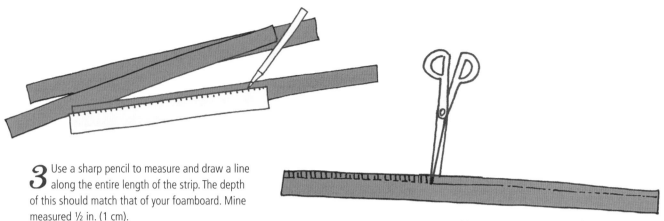

3 Use a sharp pencil to measure and draw a line along the entire length of the strip. The depth of this should match that of your foamboard. Mine measured ½ in. (1 cm).

4 Snip down to the pencil line at approximately ½ in. (1cm) intervals using a small pair of sharp scissors.

5 Fold the snipped edge over—the pencil line will act as a scored line. Line the edge of the foamboard with the colored strip and use small pieces of masking tape to stick the snipped sections to the face of the letter.

6 When you reach a curved section you may have to increase the number of strips in order to achieve a better fit.

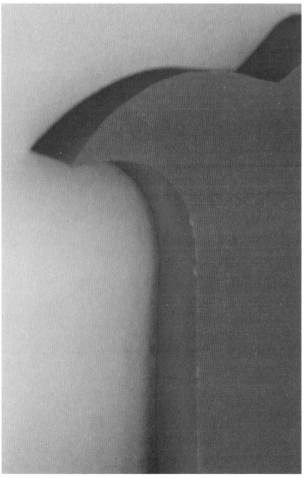

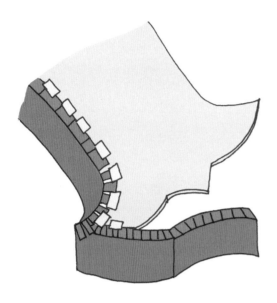

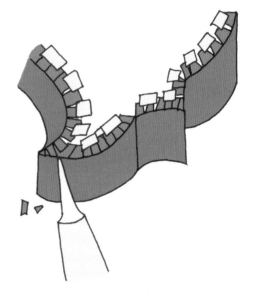

7 When you reach a corner, crease the strip neatly and continue. The snipped sections may protrude beyond the letter at pointed sections—come back to these later. Continue around the letter, adding more strips of card stock (card) as necessary. When adding a new strip, overlap the previous one by approximately ½ in. (1 cm).

8 Go back and trim any bits of card stock (card) that protrude beyond the letter shape. Use craft glue to stick these down. Also use glue to stick down any overlapping sections where a new strip has been added.

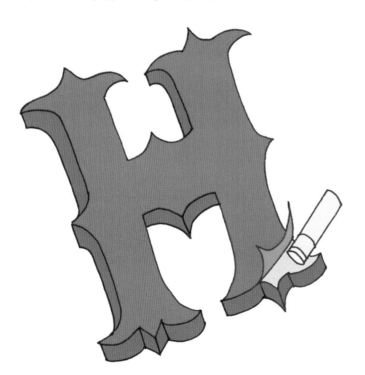

9 Trace out the letter shape again, this time onto the same colored card stock (card) as the side edges. Cut this out, cutting on the outside of the pencil mark. Spread glue over the back of the card stock (card)—this is important if your letter is not symmetrical—and stick the card stock (card) to the surface of the foamboard shape.

PRINTED LETTER ART

Look out for old printers' letter blocks in flea markets and junk shops. You can use them on all sorts of projects and they look lovely displayed on a shelf in their own right. If you can't find any, many craft stores sell rubber stamps that print very well.

YOU WILL NEED:

- Glass sheet measuring approximately 8 x 6 in. (20 x 15 cm)
- Masking tape
- Water-based printing ink in several colors
- Small lino roller
- Printers' letter blocks or rubber stamps
- White cartridge paper, measuring 16½ x 11½ in. (42 x 29.5 cm)
- Craft knife
- Cutting mat
- Ruler
- Pencil
- Thin card stock (card)
- Blunt cutlery knife for scoring
- Craft glue

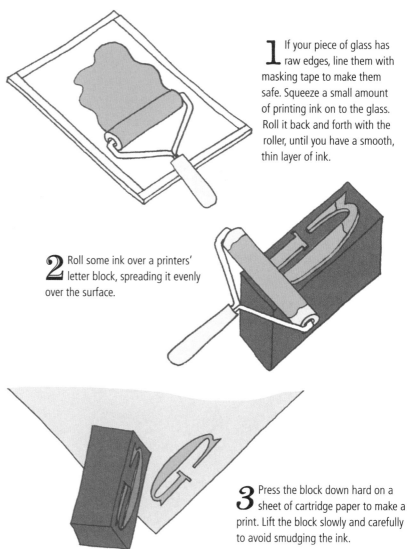

1 If your piece of glass has raw edges, line them with masking tape to make them safe. Squeeze a small amount of printing ink on to the glass. Roll it back and forth with the roller, until you have a smooth, thin layer of ink.

2 Roll some ink over a printers' letter block, spreading it evenly over the surface.

3 Press the block down hard on a sheet of cartridge paper to make a print. Lift the block slowly and carefully to avoid smudging the ink.

4 Build up your design, printing letters with different typefaces and changing the color of the ink. Make an interesting arrangement by changing the orientation of some letters and by placing big letters next to small ones.

Tips

Once you have assembled all of your materials, it makes sense to print up a large sheet of paper, but you can always use smaller pieces of paper, too.

If you are using rubber stamps, use inkpads instead of a lino roller.

Print a single letter on some posterboard (cardboard) to make a gift tag.

5 When you have covered the paper with printed letters and the ink is dry, use a craft knife to cut out some squares and rectangles for making greeting cards. Be sure to protect your work surface with a cutting mat. It doesn't matter if some of the printed letters get cut in half—they simply become part of an abstract design.

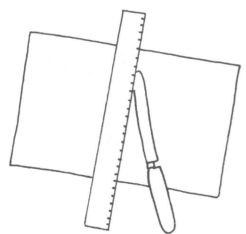

6 Measure and cut out some thin card stock (card) that is exactly twice the size of one of your shapes. Use a blunt knife to score and fold the card in half.

7 Use craft glue to stick your printed design onto the front of the folded card.

3

Mixed-media
LETTERS

WEATHERED WOOD LETTER

I'm always on the look-out for old planks of wood, especially painted ones with worn layers of color and areas of bare wood. This wooden letter is made from a plain piece of decking that has been painted and sanded down to achieve the same distressed effect. Turn this letter "N" on its side and you have a letter "Z." Two for the price of one!

YOU WILL NEED:

- Piece of wood measuring 40 x 3½ in. (1 m x 9 cm)
- Ruler
- Pencil
- Saw
- Wood glue
- Paint
- Paintbrush
- Sandpaper

1 Cut two lengths from the wood, each measuring 11 in. (28 cm). These are the uprights for the letter "N." Lay them flat on the table, with a 5½ in. (14 cm) gap between them, and their bases aligned.

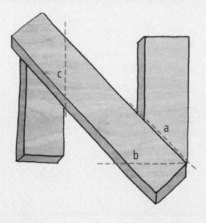

2 Lay the remaining length of wood diagonally across from the top left of the first upright to the bottom right of the second. Position it so that the bottom right corners are aligned, as shown. Mark with a pencil the three cuts you need to make, marked "a," "b," and "c" on the illustration.

3 Use a saw to cut along the pencil lines.

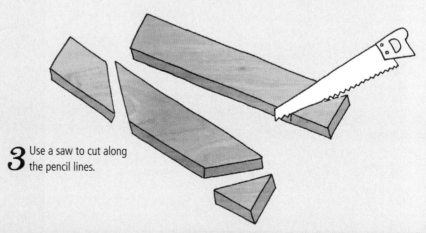

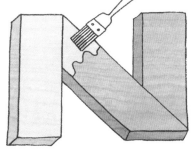

4 Use wood glue to join the three pieces together. Leave to dry.

5 Apply several layers of paint, leaving the paint to dry between each coat.

6 Use sandpaper to rub away some of the paint for a lovely distressed look.

FRUIT-CRATE LETTER

I love fruit crates! I have found many lovely boxes lying among the squashed bananas and cabbage leaves. They look great as storage boxes on open shelves and I have even been known to cover a cabinet with them. Recently I discovered that they're ideal for making letters, too—straight-sided capital letters work best (E, H, M, T, and W, for example). Look for crates with interesting graphics.

YOU WILL NEED:

- Fruit crates
- Pliers or a flat-ended screwdriver
- Staple gun or wood glue
- Utility knife (Stanley knife)
- Metal ruler

1 Use the pliers or a flat-ended screwdriver to remove the staples holding the fruit crate together. Once you have assembled a selection of wooden slats from the dismantled crate, you can start arranging them to make a letter.

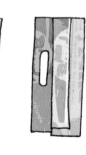

2 Overlap a number of slats to make each section of the letter. To make this "M," I used the slats to make four rectangles: two measuring 7 x 17 in. (18 x 43 cm) and two measuring 5 ½ x 12¼ in. (14 x 31 cm).

3 Use the staple gun or wood glue to join the slats for each section together.

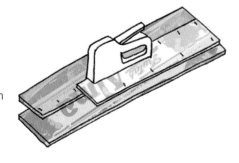

4 Protecting your work surface with a cutting mat, use the utility knife (Stanley knife) to trim each section to size, cutting against a metal ruler for a neat edge.

5 Arrange the separate sections to make your letter: here the two longer pieces form the sides of the letter and the two smaller pieces the center "V" shape. Make sure the sections overlap so that you have something to staple or glue. Use the staple gun or glue to join the pieces together.

CORRUGATED CAPITAL

You can transform a sheet of ordinary corrugated posterboard (cardboard) into a sculptural letter in a few easy steps. Plus, by cutting into the top layer of, and pressing down the corrugations, you can introduce a stylish and contemporary graphic element.

1 Choose your letter, or use the template on page 132, and enlarge it to the right size, either by using a photocopier or scaling the letter up on graph paper (see page 9). Protecting your work surface with a cutting mat, use a craft knife to cut out the shape. Trace out the letter and transfer it onto a piece of foamboard (see page 10).

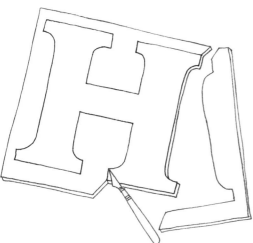

2 Cut out the shape using a craft knife and a ruler for any straight sections. Use the same method to make an identical letter from the second piece of foamboard and stick the two together using glue.

3 Place the corrugated posterboard (cardboard) on your work surface—smooth side up—and lay the foamboard letter on top. Draw around the shape and cut it out.

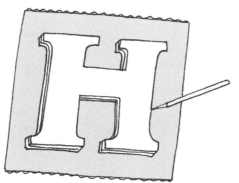

YOU WILL NEED:

- Letter template
- Plain paper or graph
- Ruler
- Pencil
- Tracing paper
- Masking tape
- 2 pieces of foamboard, each measuring 14 x 17½ in. (36 x 44 cm)
- Craft knife
- Cutting mat
- Craft glue
- Corrugated posterboard (cardboard) measuring 10¼ x 17½ in. (26 x 44 cm)
- Small scrap of thick card stock (card)
- Roll of washi tape
- Scissors

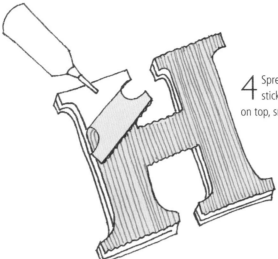

4 Spread glue all over the foamboard letter and stick the corrugated posterboard (cardboard) on top, smooth side down.

5 Trace out a triangle template measuring 3½ in. (9 cm) on the two long sides, and 1½ in. (4 cm) on the short side, transfer it onto a piece of card stock (card), and cut it out. You can now use the template to score a pattern in the corrugated posterboard (cardboard). It works best down, or along, a straight edge. For this letter "H," I scored a pattern down the left-hand edge of each upright.

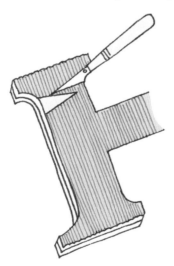

6 Starting 1¾ in. (4.5 cm) from the top of the letter on the left-hand side, position the triangle template so that the short edge is aligned with the straight edge of the letter. Run a craft knife the length of the two long sides of the triangle template, just cutting through the corrugations.

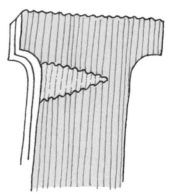

7 Push down gently on the cut shape to form an indented triangle. Repeat all the way down the straight edge of the letter.

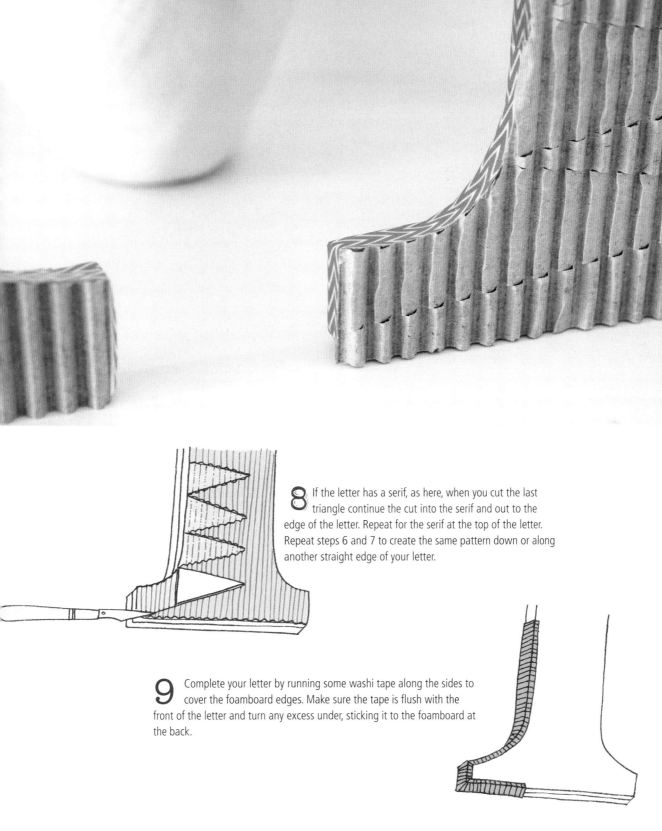

8 If the letter has a serif, as here, when you cut the last triangle continue the cut into the serif and out to the edge of the letter. Repeat for the serif at the top of the letter. Repeat steps 6 and 7 to create the same pattern down or along another straight edge of your letter.

9 Complete your letter by running some washi tape along the sides to cover the foamboard edges. Make sure the tape is flush with the front of the letter and turn any excess under, sticking it to the foamboard at the back.

STRING LETTERS

I love natural fabrics like linen and jute, so it will come as no surprise that out of the many things I collect, one of them is string. Balls of string come in many different colors and widths. They look lovely and smell nice, too! I have used two contrasting shades to make these simple and stylish letters.

1 Print out your chosen letters from a computer or take them from the templates (see page 134) and enlarge them to the desired size. I made my "O" 12 in. (30 cm) tall and the "d" 9 in. (23 cm) tall. You can either use a photocopier or scale the letter up using graph paper (see page 9). Trace out the letter and transfer it onto the posterboard (cardboard) (see page 10). Protecting your work surface with a cutting mat, use a craft knife to cut out the shapes.

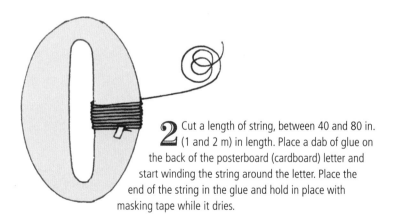

2 Cut a length of string, between 40 and 80 in. (1 and 2 m) in length. Place a dab of glue on the back of the posterboard (cardboard) letter and start winding the string around the letter. Place the end of the string in the glue and hold in place with masking tape while it dries.

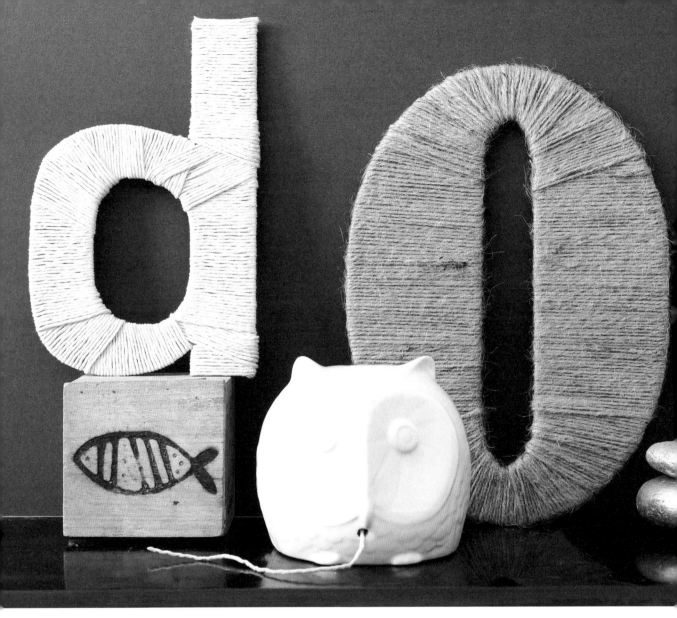

3 Keep the string neat as you continue to wind it around the letter, with each strand flat against the card and flush with the piece of string next to it. Continue to spread glue on the back of the letter as you go and secure with some masking tape if you need it.

4 When you reach a curve or serif you will need to overlap the string in places to prevent the posterboard (cardboard) showing through. I like to do this by altering the angle of the string for a section. I then cut off the string and change the angle again for the next section, so that all areas get covered. I try to do this in blocks, because it looks neat and adds a geometric, textural look to the wound string.

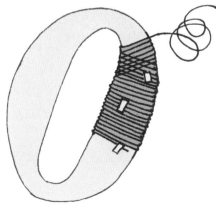

SLOT-TOGETHER LETTERS

Like my fabric stash, my collection of paper is ever increasing. I save bits of giftwrap, labels, paper bags, and bits from magazines—in fact anything that I think I could use on a project. I chose some beautiful Indian-inspired craft paper for these card stock (card) letters. They are so simple to make and would make a lovely gift for a friend. You can cover them in anything. Black-and-white photos copied onto some printer paper would work really well.

YOU WILL NEED:

- Letter and tab template
- Plain or graph paper
- Ruler
- Pencil
- Tracing paper
- Masking tape
- 2 sheets of thin card stock (card) measuring approximately 8¼ x 8¼ in. (21 x 21 cm)
- Craft knife
- Cutting mat
- Craft glue
- 2 sheets of craft paper
- Tab template (see page 135)
- ¹⁄₁₆ in. (1 mm) thick posterboard (cardboard)

1 Print out your chosen letter from a computer or take a letter from the templates (see page 135) and enlarge it to the desired size. I have made mine approximately 8 in. (20 cm) tall. You can either use a photocopier or scale the letter up using graph paper (see page 9). Trace out the letter and transfer it twice onto thin card stock (card) (see page 10). Place on a cutting mat and use a craft knife to cut them out.

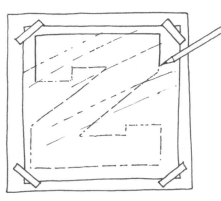

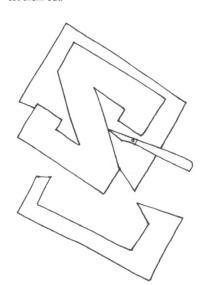

2 Spread glue all over the front of one of the letters and place a sheet of craft paper, pattern facing up, onto the letter. Press the paper down all over and allow the glue to dry before using a craft knife to trim off any excess. Repeat on the front of the second letter.

3 You now have to decide how many tabs you will need to hold your two pieces together, to make your letter three-dimensional. On my letter "Z" I have placed two tabs at the bottom and two tabs at the top. If you were making a capital "A," three tabs would be better—two at the bottom and one at the top.

4 Trace out the tab template on page 135 and cut out the number you need from the thicker posterboard (cardboard). Cover each side of a tab in the same craft paper that you used on the front of the first letter. As you finish each side, trim off the excess paper, including the slots, allowing the glue to dry first. Repeat for all your tabs.

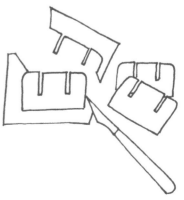

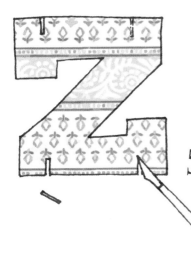

5 Mark, in pencil, the position of the corresponding slots on the front of the first letter. They need to be ½ in. (1 cm) tall and just over 1 mm wide. (If you are using a different thickness of card, the slots on your letter and on the tabs should be just slightly over the measurement of the width of your card.) I have positioned my tabs 1½ in. (4 cm) in from each edge at the top and bottom of the letter. Cut the slots out of the letter.

6 Place the front letter over the second letter, aligning the bases together but shifting the top letter to the left by ½ in. (1 cm). Use a sharp pencil to mark out the slots through the top letter and onto the lower letter.

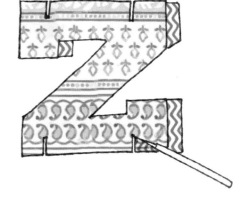

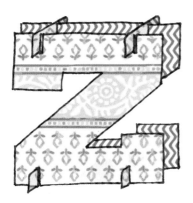

7 Cut out the slots on the lower letter. To join your letters together, push the tabs into position. Be sure to push them in firmly, so that the edge of the letter is flush with the top of the tab.

Tips

These letters look best when they're nice and sturdy, so make sure you have enough connecting tabs holding everything in place.

Why not make some extra-large versions of these letters to decorate your home? They will make such a bold impact and as they can stand up on their own, you can put them anywhere.

COFFEE SACK LETTERS

Coffee shops often have sacks to give away. I like them for their printed lettering and graphics. They make a great background for some boldly stitched letters. If you can't get hold of any sacks, buy some sacking from a fabric shop and use a brightly colored backing fabric for contrast. Choose a thick fabric—canvas would work well.

1 Cut out an oblong of sacking from the coffee sack. Mine measures approximately 12 x 12½ in. (30 x 32 cm)—there is no need to be precise. Cut a second piece from different material, making is slightly bigger all around than the first piece.

2 Choose your first letter, or use the template on page 135, and enlarge it to the right size, either by using a photocopier or scaling the letter up on graph paper (see page 9). I made mine approximately 9 in. (23 cm) tall. Trace out the letter and use scissors to cut out the shape so that you can use it as a paper template (see page 10).

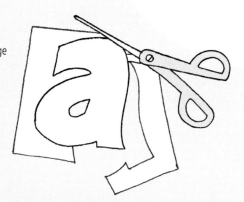

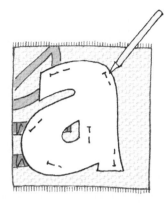

3 Center the letter template on the smaller piece of sacking, right side up, and pin in place, and use a felt-tip pen to draw around it.

4 Place the smaller piece of sacking on top of the larger piece—both right side up. The larger piece will give the smaller piece a border, but do not worry about getting this perfectly equal all the way around. It is nice to have random widths. Pin the two pieces together.

5 Set your sewing machine to a wide, but tight, zigzag and sew over the pen lines to make the letter.

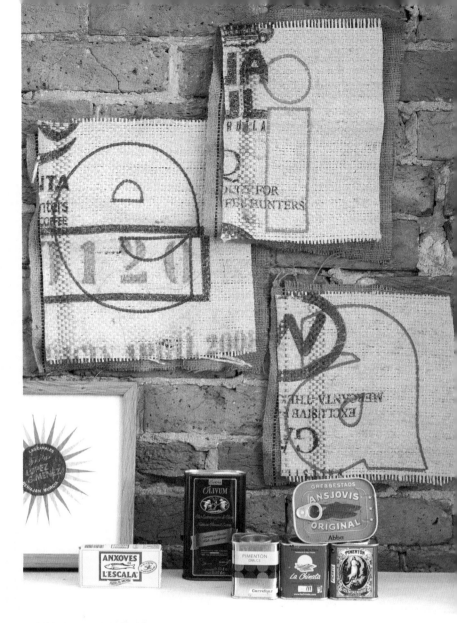

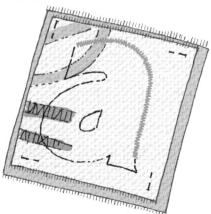

CONCRETE CAPITAL

I chose a letter with only straight parts for this project, as I think one with curved sections would be a challenge too far! However, concrete is much easier to work with than you might think. I used wood taken from some old fruit crates to make the mold, as it is easy to cut the wood using a utility knife (Stanley knife).

YOU WILL NEED:

- Sections of wood from an old fruit crate
- Ruler
- Pencil
- Utility knife (Stanley knife)
- Cutting mat
- Duct tape
- Wooden board measuring approximately 20 x 20 in. (50 x 50 cm)
- Easy-mix concrete
- Old bucket

1 Using a utility knife (Stanley knife), and protecting your work surface with a cutting mat, cut the lengths of wood you need. For my letter "A," I used the following lengths (see diagram): Two x 14 in. (35 cm), two x 4 in. (10 cm), two x 3¼ in. (8.5 cm), two x 3 in. (8 cm), one x 5 in. (12.5 cm), one x 2⅞ in. (7.5 cm), and one x 2½ in. (6.5 cm). Each of my sections was approximately 4 in. (10 cm) in width (see diagram).

2¼ in. (7.5 cm)
3 in. (8 cm)
14 in. (35 cm)
2½ in. (6.5 cm)
5 in. (12.5 cm)
3¼ in. (8.5 cm)
4 in. (10 cm)

2 Start constructing the mold by joining the pieces of wood together to form the letter—in this case, an "A." Join one long side to the top section applying some duct tape where the corners meet. Now join the second long side in the same way and so on, until you have made the outside shape of the letter. Make up the small, inner triangle section in the same way.

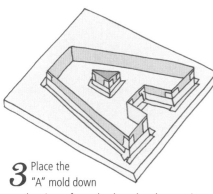

3 Place the "A" mold down on the piece of wooden board and secure in place using duct tape. Make sure that there are no gaps through which the wet concrete might seep. Position the inner triangle section and secure firmly using more tape.

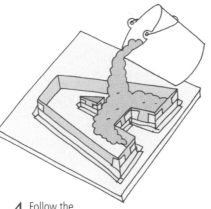

4 Follow the instructions to make the easy-mix concrete in a bucket. Pour the concrete into the mold and smooth over the top.

5 Leave to dry. This may take a few days. Be patient, because if you take it out too early, the shape may crack. When the concrete is completely dry you can dismantle the wooden mold and stand the letter up.

LIGHT IT UP

Friends of mine bought a vintage light-up letter in a flea market a few years ago. I have always admired it and set out to make a light-up letter of my own. Constructed from yellow card, the result is a vibrant statement piece even when not switched on.

YOU WILL NEED:

- Yellow mounting board measuring 19 x 23½ in. (48 x 60 cm)
- Pencil
- Ruler
- String
- Masking tape
- Thumbtack (drawing pin)
- Triangle (set square)
- White mounting board measuring 21¼ x 26¾ in. (54 x 68 cm)
- Craft knife
- Cutting mat
- Craft glue
- Drill with ⅛ in. (3 mm) drill bit
- String of 20 battery-operated LED lights

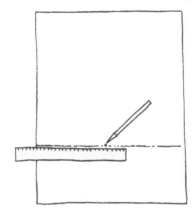

1 Place the yellow mounting board face down on your work surface. I have chosen to make my light-up letter in the shape of a "U." Measure up 11 in. (28 cm) from the bottom of the board and use a pencil and ruler to draw a horizontal line across the board at this point. Mark the center point along the line.

2 Cut a length of string measuring approximately 12 in. (30 cm). Attach one end of the string close to the bottom of a pencil, using a small piece of masking tape.

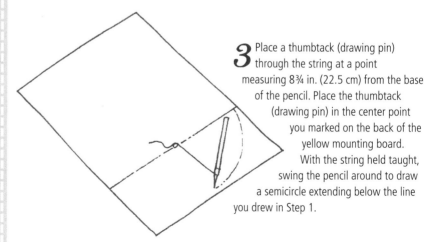

3 Place a thumbtack (drawing pin) through the string at a point measuring 8¾ in. (22.5 cm) from the base of the pencil. Place the thumbtack (drawing pin) in the center point you marked on the back of the yellow mounting board. With the string held taught, swing the pencil around to draw a semicircle extending below the line you drew in Step 1.

4 Now place the thumbtack (drawing pin) at 3 in. (7.5 cm) along the string and repeat Step 3 to draw a smaller semicircle within the larger one.

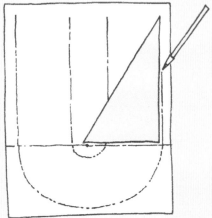

5 Using a triangle (set square), extend the stems of the letter "U," 12½ in. (32 cm) up from the tops of your two semicircles. Draw in a horizontal line at the top of each stem to complete the "U" shape.

6 Repeat Steps 1 to 5 to draw a larger "U" on the white mounting board, using the following measurements: baseline: 11 in. (28 cm) up from the bottom of the board; string length: 12 in. (30 cm); string length for outer semicircle: 10½ in. (26.5 cm); string length for inner semicircle: 1½ in. (4 cm); letter stem height 14¼ in. (36 cm).

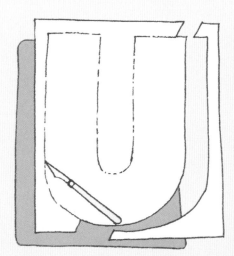

7 Protecting your work surface with a cutting mat, use a craft knife to cut out the two shapes. Mounting board is thick and quite hard to cut. Make sure your blade is sharp so that it does not slip. Cut carefully and slowly.

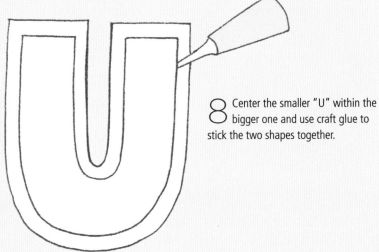

8 Center the smaller "U" within the bigger one and use craft glue to stick the two shapes together.

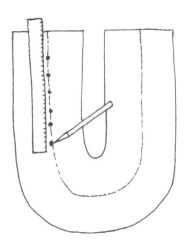

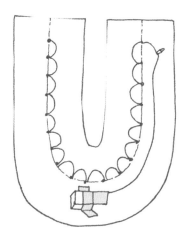

9 On the back of the larger "U," measure and mark a pencil line at the center of the letter, as shown. Starting on one side, mark a dot on the line, 2¼ in. (6 cm) down from the top edge of the letter. Continue to mark the line at 2¼ in. (6 cm) intervals. This will give you 19 dots.

10 Use a ⅛ in. (3 mm) drill bit to make holes where you made the dots in Step 9 —these are for your lightbulbs. They should fit snugly. If your bulbs are bigger, adjust the drill bit accordingly. Push the bulbs through the holes and secure the battery pack to the back of your light-up letter using masking tape.

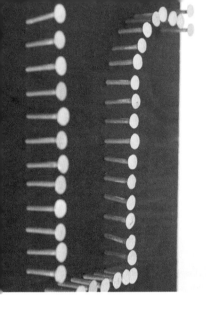

NAILED OUTLINE

You don't need expensive materials to make stylish letters. I have made this letter "r" using a few nails hammered into an offcut of wood. For an alternative look, use brightly colored thumbtacks (drawing pins) stuck into a piece of painted wood.

YOU WILL NEED:

- Letter template
- Plain or graph paper
- Ruler
- Pencil
- Tracing paper
- Masking tape
- Scissors
- Wood measuring
  12½ x 7¾ in. x 1½ in.
  (32 x 20 x 3.5 cm)
- Awl
- Nails
- Hammer

1 Choose a letter, or use the template on page 137, and enlarge it to the right size, either by using a photocopier or by scaling the letter up on graph paper (see page 9). My letter measured approximately 9 in. (22 cm) in height. Transfer your letter onto tracing paper (see page 10).

2 Use a pencil to mark the letter outline with dots at ½ in. (1 cm) intervals. Your shape may not divide exactly by this measurement, so space out the last four or five dots to fill the remaining space evenly. Use scissors to cut your letter shape out, making sure you can still see the marked dots.

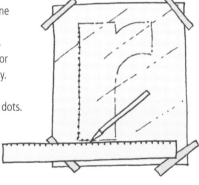

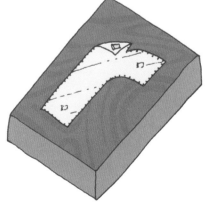

3 Center the traced letter on the piece of wood. Roll small pieces of masking tape into tubes and stick these beneath the letter to hold it in place.

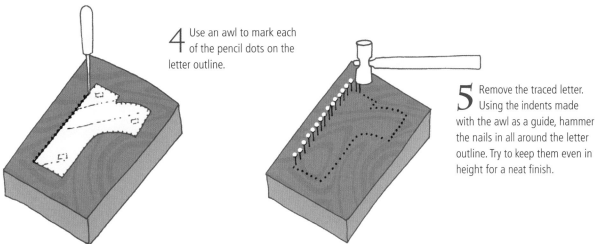

4 Use an awl to mark each of the pencil dots on the letter outline.

5 Remove the traced letter. Using the indents made with the awl as a guide, hammer the nails in all around the letter outline. Try to keep them even in height for a neat finish.

INDUSTRIAL-STYLE CUTOUTS

These stencil cutouts are made from thick card stock (card) then painted and sprayed. Adding some sand to the paint mix gives the finished piece a wonderful textural surface. Follow this with a few coats of metallic spray for a contemporary industrial finish.

YOU WILL NEED:

- Letter template
- Plain or graph paper
- Ruler
- Pencil
- Tracing paper
- Masking tape
- Card stock (card) measuring 7½ x 6 in. (19 x 15 cm)
- Craft knife
- Cutting mat
- Dark-red acrylic paint
- Sand
- Bowl
- Tablespoon
- Metallic paint spray
- Newspaper

1 Choose a letter from a stencil typeface, or use the templates on page 136, and enlarge it to the right size, either by using a photocopier or by scaling the letter up on graph paper (see page xx). My letter measured approximately 4¾ in. (12 cm) in height.

2 Trace out the letter and transfer it onto a piece of card stock (card) (see page 10). Cut out the shape using a craft knife, remembering to protect your work surface with a cutting mat.

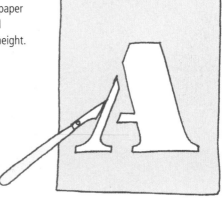

3 In a bowl, mix a few squeezes of the acrylic paint with approximately one heaped tablespoonful of sand.

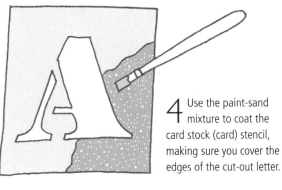

4 Use the paint-sand mixture to coat the card stock (card) stencil, making sure you cover the edges of the cut-out letter.

5 When the paint-sand coating is dry, spray the card stock (card) with metallic paint. I used "pewter." You should do this outside and on newspaper. Once the first coat of metallic paint has dried give it another. With spray paint it is always best to use several thin coats rather than one thick one.

WIRE CAGE LETTER

I like to experiment with different materials to get different looks. I hadn't used galvanized wire before, but love the industrial look of metal letters, so gave it a go. I was pleased with the result. Be very careful when you cut the wire as it is sharp. Always use a pair of pliers to bend the wire, never your fingers.

YOU WILL NEED:

- Letter template
- Plain or graph paper
- Ruler
- Pencil
- Tracing paper
- Masking tape
- Scissors
- Sheet of ½ in. (1 cm) grid galvanized wire measuring 40 x 20 in. (100 x 50 cm)
- Felt-tip pen
- Wire cutters
- Pliers

1 Print out your chosen letter from a computer or use the template on page 136 and enlarge it to the desired size. Mine measured 13 x 10 in. (34 x 25 cm). You can either use a photocopier or scale the letter up using graph paper (see page 9). Trace out the letter and transfer it onto paper (see page 10). Use scissors to cut out the shape.

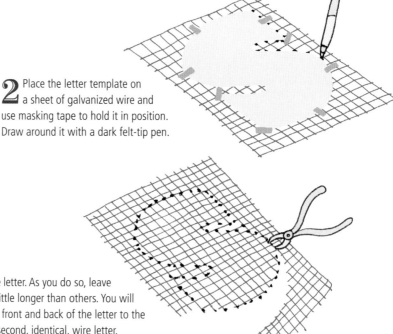

2 Place the letter template on a sheet of galvanized wire and use masking tape to hold it in position. Draw around it with a dark felt-tip pen.

3 Use wire cutters to cut out the letter. As you do so, leave some of the trimmed wires a little longer than others. You will use these later, when attaching the front and back of the letter to the sides. Use the template to make a second, identical, wire letter.

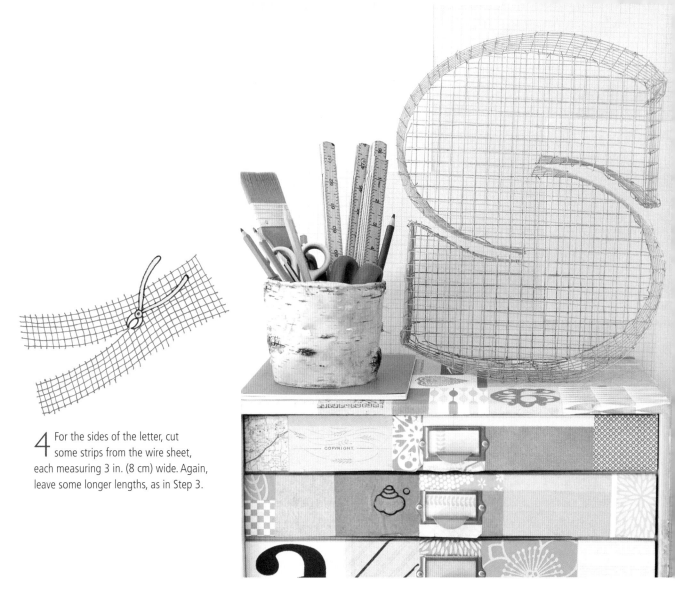

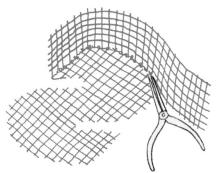

4 For the sides of the letter, cut some strips from the wire sheet, each measuring 3 in. (8 cm) wide. Again, leave some longer lengths, as in Step 3.

5 Place the first letter shape, right side down, on your work surface. Align a side strip at right angles to the edge of the front letter. Working your way around the perimeter of the front letter, use pliers to bend the longer lengths of wire over the edges of the side strip and vice versa, to secure them tightly.

6 Continue to add lengths of side strips, bending them into shape as you work them around any corners or curves.

7 Attach the second letter shape in the same way.

4

Fabric

LETTERS

VINTAGE FABRIC LETTER

A friend of mine gave me a vintage floral curtain some time ago and it has been sitting with my stash of fabric ever since, just waiting to be made into something. I thought it would be perfect for this pretty fabric letter. I have used a contrasting fabric on the reverse, making the letter double sided.

YOU WILL NEED:

- Letter template
- Plain or graph paper
- Ruler
- Pencil
- Tracing paper
- Masking tape
- Piece of foamboard measuring 13 x 11 in. (33 x 28 cm)
- Craft knife
- Cutting mat
- 2 pieces of fabric, each measuring 13¾ x 15¾ in. (35 x 40 cm)
- Scissors
- A piece of thick batting (wadding) measuring 13 x 11 in (33 x 28 cm)
- Felt-tip pen
- Pins
- Sewing needle and thread

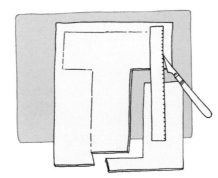

1 Choose a letter or use the template on page 136 and enlarge it to the desired size. You can either use a photocopier or scale the letter up using graph paper (see page 9). Trace the letter out and transfer it on to a piece of foamboard (see page 10). Use a craft knife and ruler to cut it out.

2 Lay the fabric you want to use for the front of your letter on your work surface, right side up. Place your letter shape on top (again right side up). This way you can see how the pattern falls within your letter. Draw around the shape of the letter approximately 1 in. (2.5 cm) away from the edge of the letter. Use scissors to cut the shape out. Do the same for the fabric you have chosen for the back, but this time place the letter shape right side down (so the letter is reversed) and leave a ½ in. (15 mm) border.

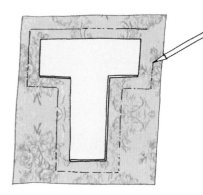

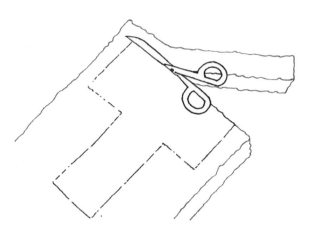

3 Place the letter shape on the piece of batting (wadding) and draw round the edge of it. It is quite hard to draw on the fluffy surface, so use a felt-tip pen. The batting (wadding) should be the same size as the foamboard, with no border. Use scissors to cut the shape out.

4 Lay the fabric for the front of the letter right side down on your work surface. Place the batting (wadding) on top of it, and the foamboard letter on top of the batting (wadding). Begin to fold the fabric over the edges of the foamboard and secure it to the back using masking tape. Try to keep the border the same width all the way around and pull the fabric smooth as you go. Where your letter has a corner, snip into the fabric at a 45-degree angle and pull the fabric as close into the corner as you can.

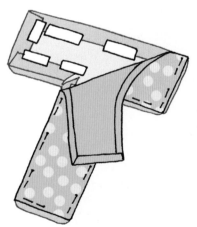

5 With the letter face down on your work surface, pin the backing fabric onto the back of it. Turn under a hem as you move around the shape of the letter and push pins though the overlapping fabric from the front piece of fabric.

6 Use small appliqué stitches to secure the backing fabric in place. You may find a curved needle easier to use. When you come to a corner, pull the fabric in as much as you can, and secure with more stitches to hide any raw edges.

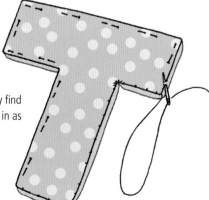

MIX-IT-UP FABRIC MAGNETS

I have used scraps of bright fabric to make these little letters. They are so simple to make, it wouldn't take long to sew a whole alphabet. Attach magnets to their backs, stick them on to the refrigerator door and make learning the ABC more fun!

1 Choose your letter, or use the templates on page 138 and enlarge it to the right size, either by using a photocopier or by scaling the letter up on graph paper (see page 9). I have made mine approximately 4 in. (10 cm) in height. Use a nice chunky typeface, as this will make the shape easier to stuff. Transfer the letter onto some tracing paper (see page 10) and cut out using scissors.

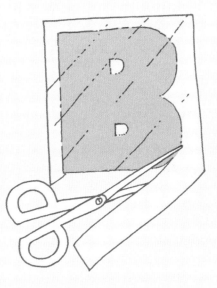

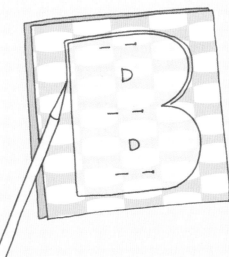

2 Cut two pieces from fabric, each slightly bigger than the letter shape. Pin them together, wrong sides facing. Pin the letter shape to the fabric and draw around it using an air erasable pen or similar.

YOU WILL NEED:

- Letter template
- Plain or graph paper
- Ruler
- Pencil
- Tracing paper
- Scissors
- Scraps of fabric
- Pins
- Air-erasable pen
- Sewing machine
- Colored sewing thread
- Soft-toy fiberfill (stuffing)
- Self-adhesive magnetic strip
- Craft glue (optional)

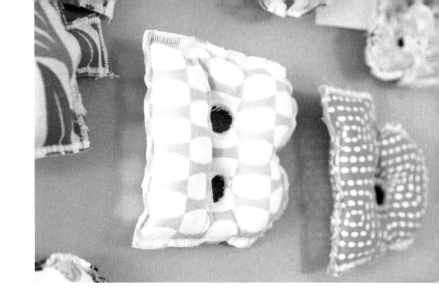

3 Sew over the drawn letter outline using a close zigzag stitch, and leaving a 1 in. (2.5 cm) gap down one side of the letter.

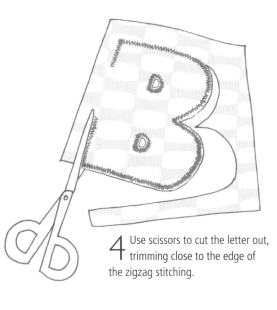

4 Use scissors to cut the letter out, trimming close to the edge of the zigzag stitching.

5 Stuff the letter with some fiberfill (stuffing), but don't overfill it. You may find it helpful to use a pencil or knitting needle to push the fiberfill (stuffing) into all the tight corners. Sew the gap closed using zigzag stitch.

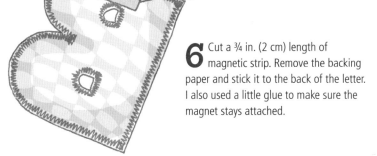

6 Cut a ¾ in. (2 cm) length of magnetic strip. Remove the backing paper and stick it to the back of the letter. I also used a little glue to make sure the magnet stays attached.

Tip

This is a great make-do-and-mend project to use up scraps of fabric that you may have left over from other craft projects.

APPLIQUÉ WALL HANGING

I have a collection of pretty scraps of fabric, embroidered napkins, bits of lace, and trimmings that come in handy for projects like this. For this attractive wall hanging, I have combined paper and fabric, but if you wanted to make yours into a pillow cover, use only fabric, buttons, and trimmings—materials that can be washed in a machine.

YOU WILL NEED:

- Letter template
- Plain or graph paper
- Ruler
- Pencil
- Tracing paper
- Masking tape
- Scissors
- Fabric measuring approximately 17½ x 17½ in. (44 x 44 cm)
- Pins
- Air-erasable pen
- Scraps of fabric and paper
- Sewing machine
- Ribbons, buttons, and charms
- Fabric tape
- Sewing needle and thread
- Thin wooden dowel measuring 17½ in. (44 cm) in length
- String

1 Choose your letter, or use the templates on page 139, and enlarge it to the right size, either by using a photocopier or by scaling the letter up on graph paper (see page 9). I chose a chunky typeface and made the letter approximately 14 in. (35 cm) in height. Transfer the letter onto some tracing paper (see page 10).

2 Use scissors to cut the letter out. Pin the letter to the piece of fabric and draw around it with the air-erasable pen or similar.

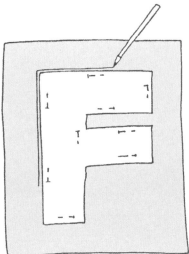

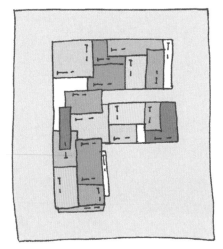

3 Use your pretty fabric and paper scraps to cover the letter shape, pinning them in place once you have an arrangement you like.

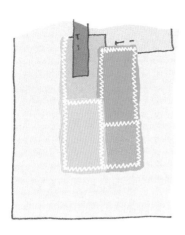

4 Use zigzag stitch on a sewing machine to secure each scrap in place.

5 Embellish the appliqué letter with lengths of ribbon, buttons, and charms.

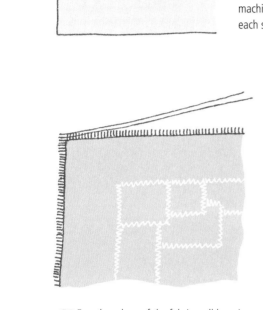

6 Fray the edges of the fabric wall hanging all the way around. You can do this by pulling away the threads that make up the fabric—up to approximately ⅓ in. (8 mm).

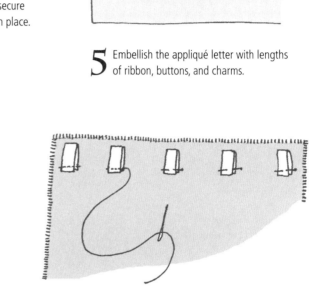

7 Cut five pieces of fabric tape, each measuring 2 in. (5 cm) in length. Fold each in half vertically to make a loop. Pin to the back of the fabric, spaced evenly across its width and with the raw ends approximately 1½ in. (4 cm) down from the top. Using small stitches, sew the raw ends of the loops to the fabric. Take care not to go all the way through the fabric, to prevent the stitches showing on the front of the wall hanging.

8 Thread the wooden dowel through the loops and tie a length of string to each end of the rod, to use for hanging.

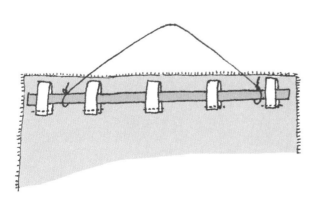

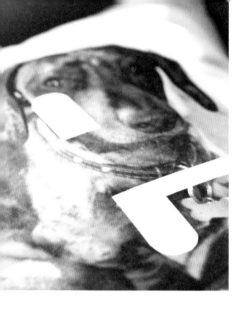

PHOTO TRANSFER

Transform a plain pillow cover with one of your favorite pictures. Photo-transfer paper, for use with an inkjet printer, is available everywhere. It is so easy to use and the results are amazing. This would make a great wedding or anniversary gift.

1 Follow the manufacturer's instructions to print your photo onto photo-transfer paper.

2 Choose a letter or use the template on page 139 and enlarge it to the right size for the pillow cover, either by using a photocopier or by scaling the letter up on graph paper (see page 9). Choose a wide typeface to show as much as possible of your photo.

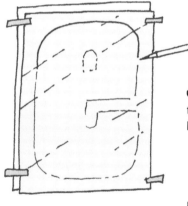

3 Trace out your letter and transfer it to the removable backing of the photo-transfer paper (see page 10). Make sure the letter faces the right way and is not reversed.

4 Protecting your work surface with a cutting mat, use a craft knife to cut out the letter.

5 Place the cut-out letter image-side down onto the pillow cover, positioning it in the center of the fabric. Follow the manufacturer's instructions to iron on the image, pressing down evenly and firmly. It usually takes a minute or two. You will be able to tell when it is time to remove the backing paper, as it starts to lift up of its own accord.

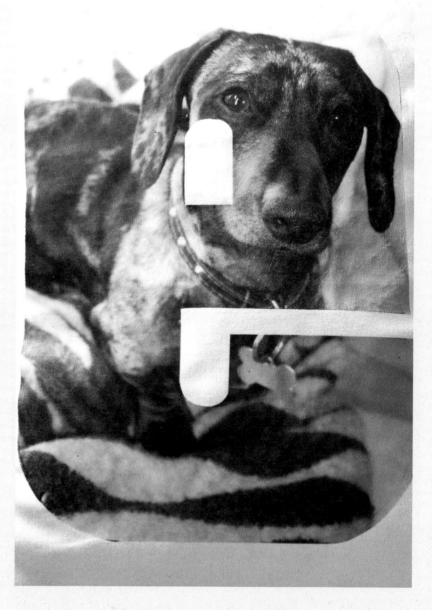

6 Carefully peel off the backing paper to reveal the image.

STUDDED JACKET

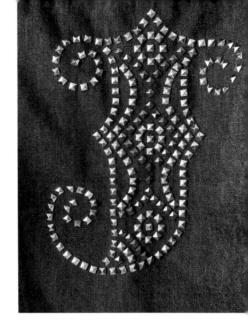

Customize an item of clothing that'll make you stand out in the crowd. For this project, I've transformed a classic denim jacket using a gorgeous decorative letter made from a combination of bronze, pewter, and chrome studs. You will be a walking work of art!

.

1 If you are using the "J" template on page 140, enlarge it to the right size for the jacket, either by using a photocopier or by scaling the letter up on graph paper (see page 9). Transfer the letter onto some tracing paper (see page 10), marking the position of each stud with a dot.

2 If you are going to make up your own letter, find one that you like, enlarge it to the right size, and transfer it to tracing paper. Using the "J" template as a guide, experiment with your design, using simple pencil lines to start with. Once satisfied, use colored pens (one for each kind of stud) to make dots ½ in. (1 cm) apart all along the pencil lines. Be sure to mark out the positions of the studs all around the edge of the letter. Adjust as necessary to avoid any big gaps or tightly bunched studs.

YOU WILL NEED:

- Letter template
- Plain or graph paper
- Pencil
- Tracing paper
- Masking tape
- Colored pens
- Awl
- Cutting mat
- Scissors
- Denim jacket
- Masking tape
- Black felt-tip pen
- Studs (they come in packs of 100; I used one x bronze, one x pewter and two x chrome packs)

3 Use an awl to punch through your tracing paper at each marked dot. Use a cutting mat to protect your work surface as you do this.

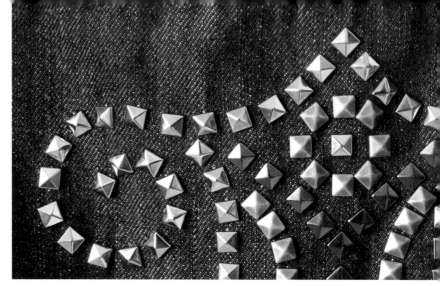

4 Use scissors to cut around the traced letter, then center it on the back of the denim jacket. Secure with some masking tape.

5 Mark through each hole in the trace using a black felt-tip pen. Don't worry about marking the jacket—the ink will be covered by the studs. Move the masking tape around to achieve the whole design.

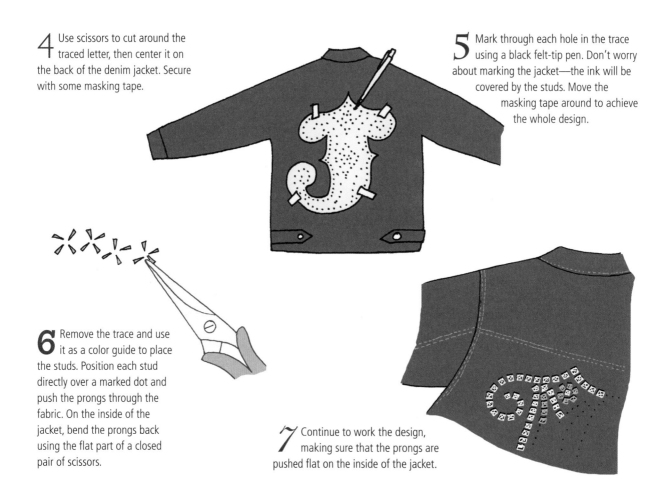

6 Remove the trace and use it as a color guide to place the studs. Position each stud directly over a marked dot and push the prongs through the fabric. On the inside of the jacket, bend the prongs back using the flat part of a closed pair of scissors.

7 Continue to work the design, making sure that the prongs are pushed flat on the inside of the jacket.

TEMPLATES

Each template is clearly marked at the percentage of actual size that it is printed, so you will need to enlarge it to the size it is to be used at. For example, if a template is marked as being 25% of actual size, this means that it is a quarter of its actual size and will need to be increased by 400% (four times its size). To do this, enlarge by 200% on a photocopier, and then enlarge that photocopy by another 200%. If a template is 50% of actual size, then it is half of its actual size and will need to be enlarged by 200%.

Silver Leaf Letter (pages 34–35)
at 25% actual size, enarge by 400%

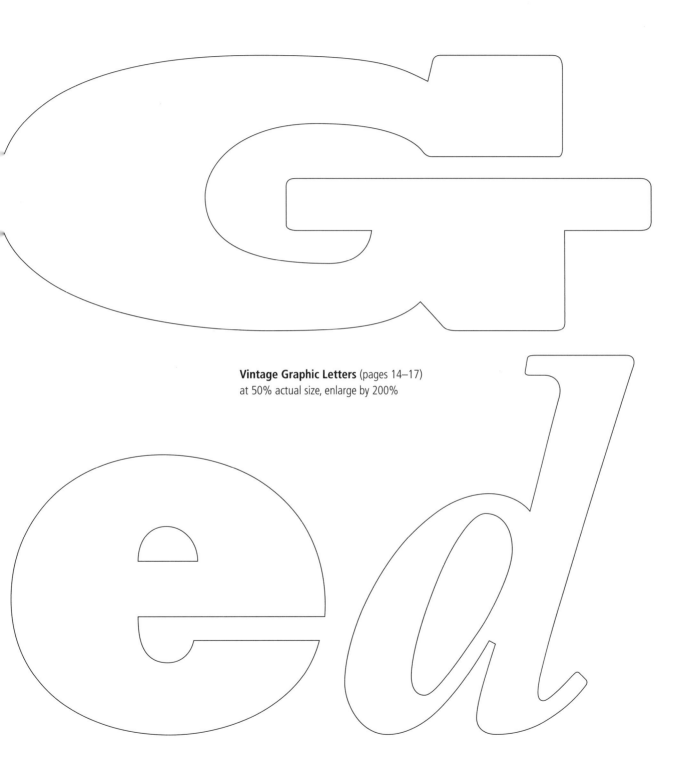

Vintage Graphic Letters (pages 14–17)
at 50% actual size, enlarge by 200%

Mexican Paper Letters (pages 36–38)
at 50% actual size, enlarge by 200%

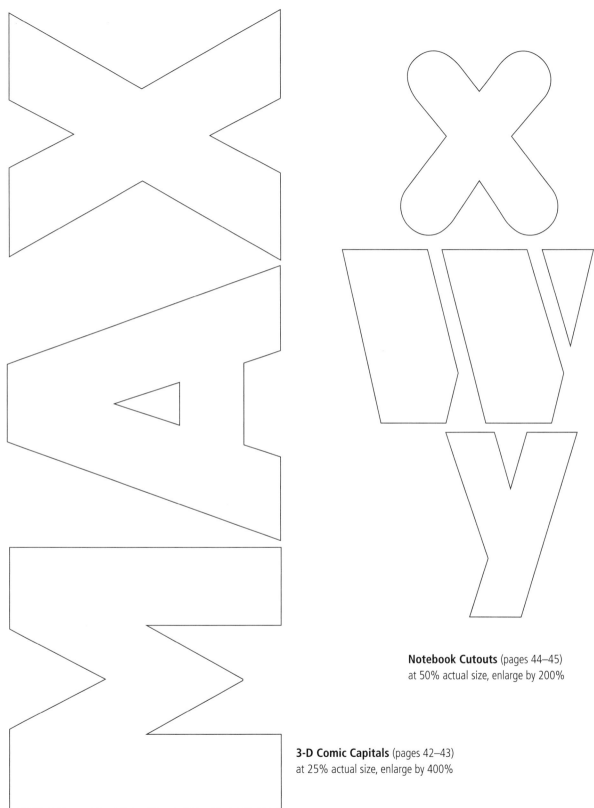

Notebook Cutouts (pages 44–45)
at 50% actual size, enlarge by 200%

3-D Comic Capitals (pages 42–43)
at 25% actual size, enlarge by 400%

Templates **127**

Simple Punched Lampshade (pages 46–47)
actual size, does not need to be enlarged

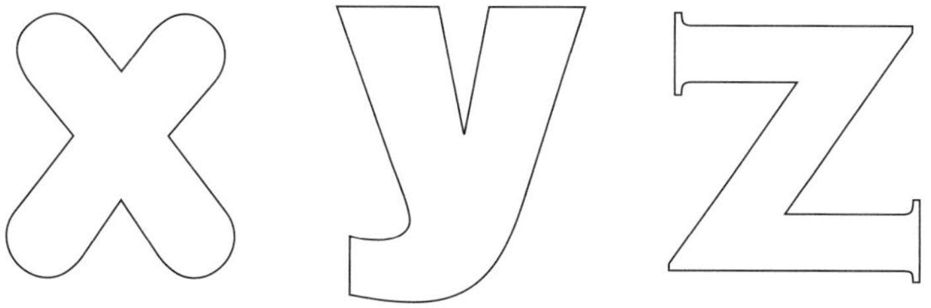

abcdef

Ghijk

LmNO

Pqrs

tuvw

xyz

Alphabet Garland (pages 48–49)
at 25% actual size, enlarge by 400%

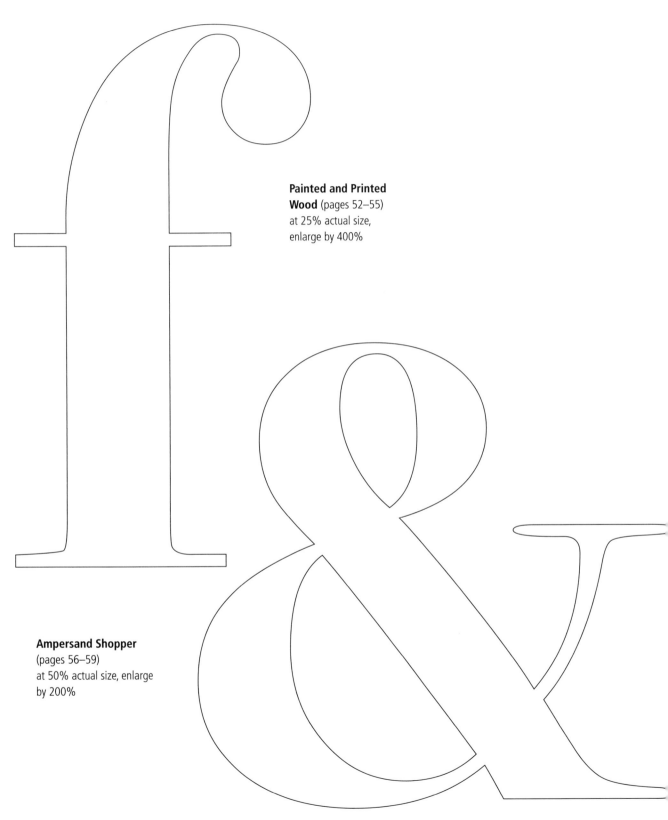

Painted and Printed Wood (pages 52–55) at 25% actual size, enlarge by 400%

Ampersand Shopper (pages 56–59) at 50% actual size, enlarge by 200%

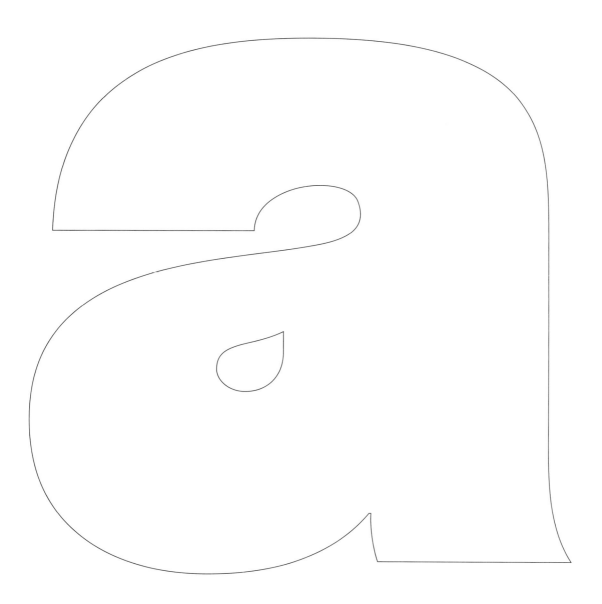

Letter-shaped Blackboard (pages 63–65)
at 25% actual size, enlarge by 400%

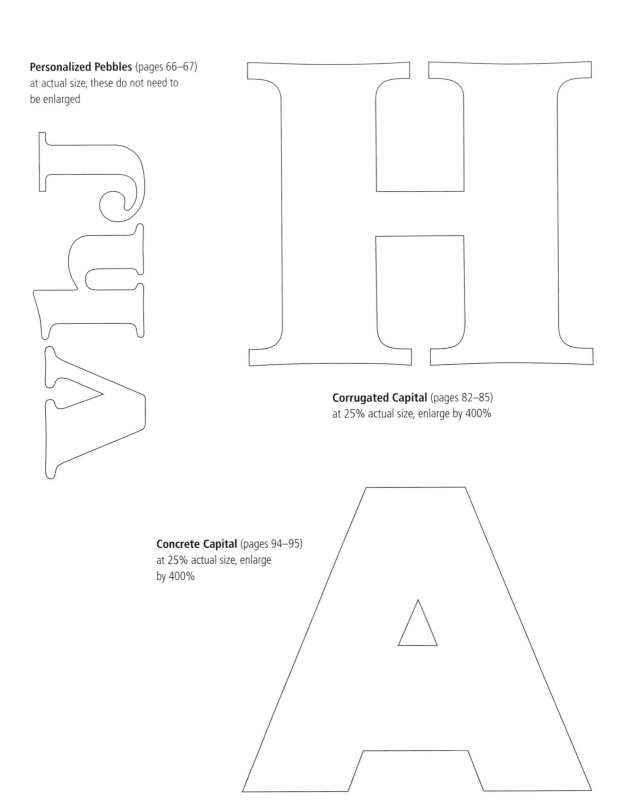

Personalized Pebbles (pages 66–67) at actual size, these do not need to be enlarged

Corrugated Capital (pages 82–85) at 25% actual size, enlarge by 400%

Concrete Capital (pages 94–95) at 25% actual size, enlarge by 400%

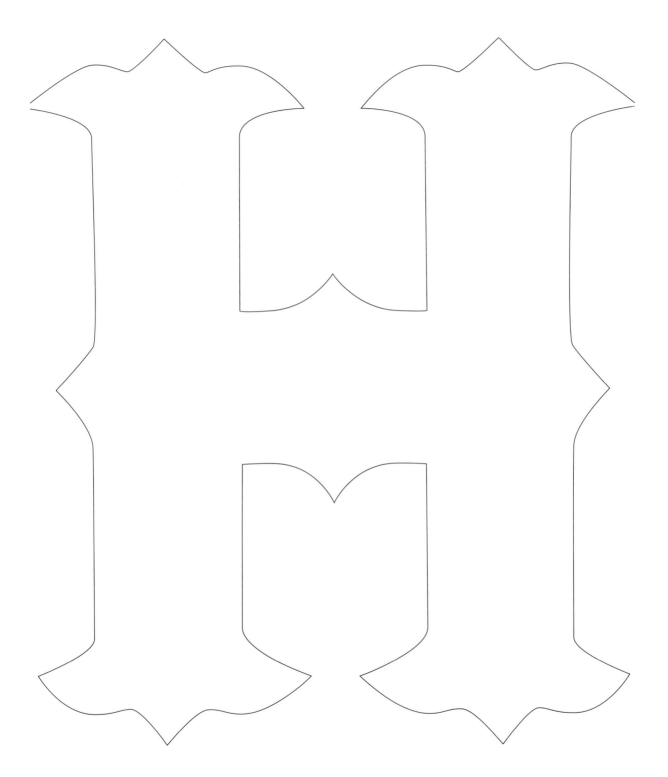

Fairground Flair (pages 68–71)
at 50% actual size, enlarge by 200%

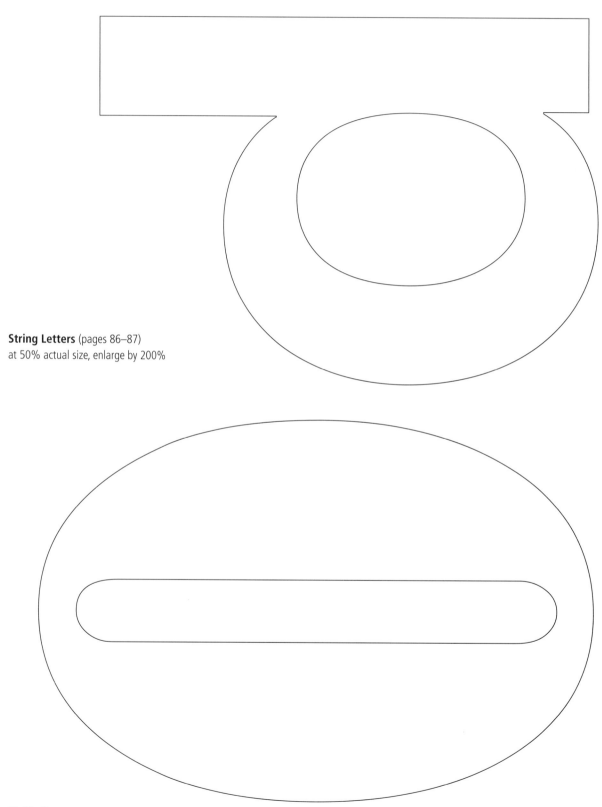

String Letters (pages 86–87)
at 50% actual size, enlarge by 200%

Slot-together Letters (pages 88–91)
at 25% actual size, enlarge by 400%

Slot-together Letters tab
(pages 88–91)
at actual size, this does not need to
be enlarged

Coffee Sack Letters (pages 92–93)
at 25% actual size, enlarge by 400%

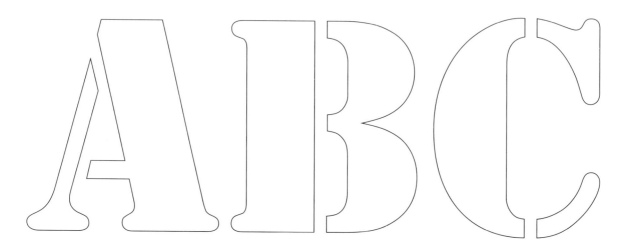

Industrial-style Cutouts (pages 102–103)
at 50% actual size, enlarge by 200%

Foamboard Lollipop Letters (pages 30–33)
at 25% actual size, enlarge by 400%

Vintage Fabric Letter (pages 108–110)
at 25% actual size, enlarge by 400%

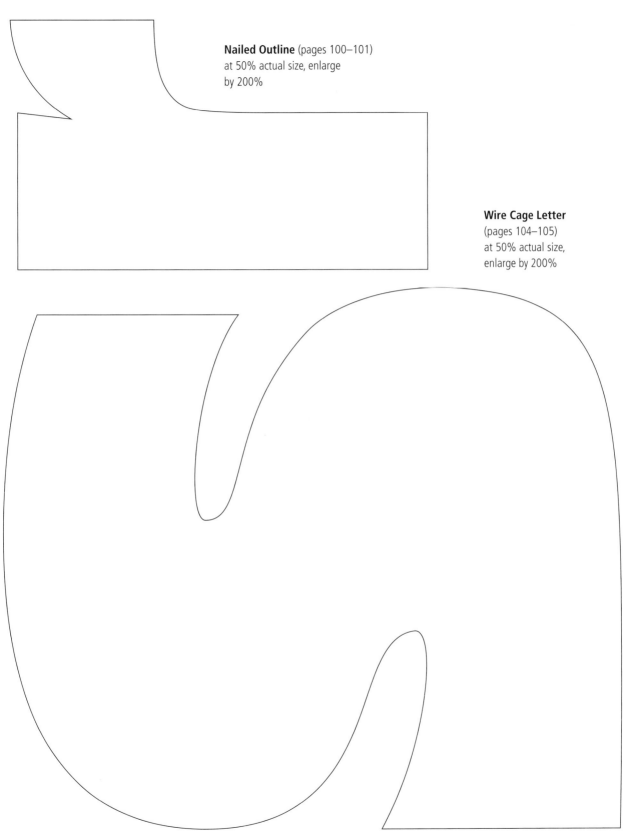

Nailed Outline (pages 100–101) at 50% actual size, enlarge by 200%

Wire Cage Letter (pages 104–105) at 50% actual size, enlarge by 200%

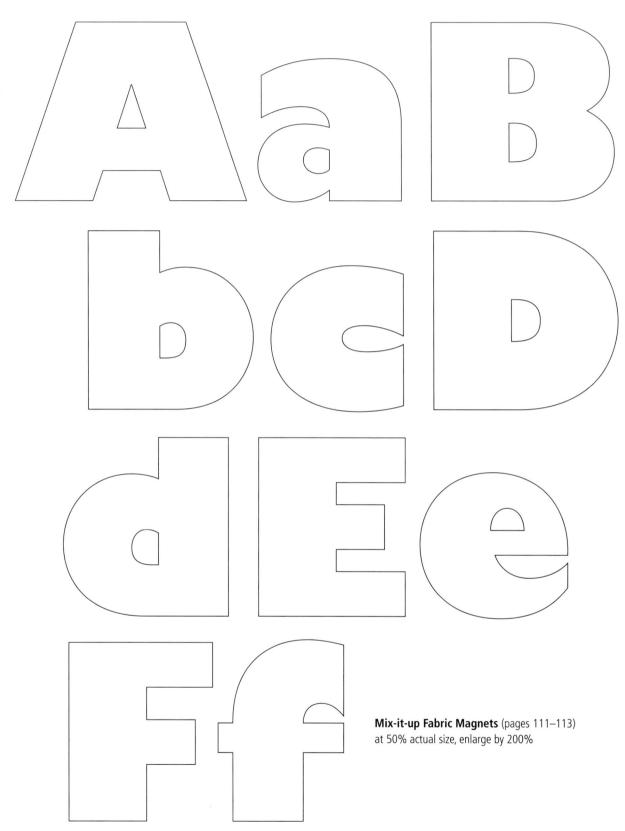

Mix-it-up Fabric Magnets (pages 111–113)
at 50% actual size, enlarge by 200%

Appliqué Wall Hanging (pages 114–117)
at 25% actual size, enlarge by 400%

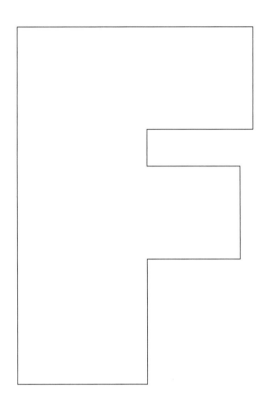

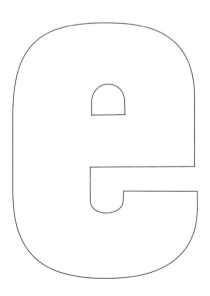

Photo Transfer (pages 118–120)
at 25% actual size, enlarge by 400%

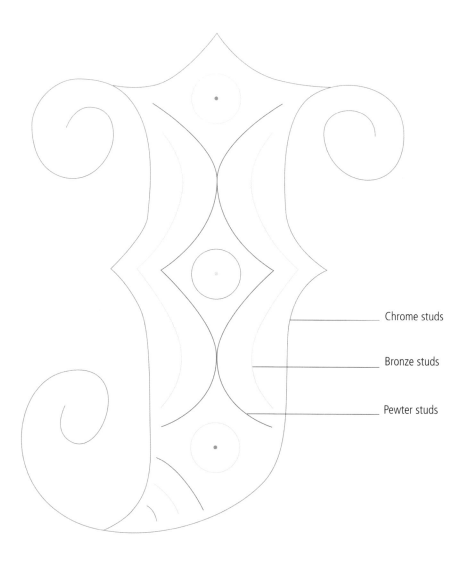

Chrome studs

Bronze studs

Pewter studs

Studded Jacket (pages 122–123)
at 50% actual size, enlarge by 200%

SUPPLIERS

US STOCKISTS

A.C. Moore
Stores nationwide
1–888–226–6673
www.acmoore.com

Craft Gate Art & Craft Directory
Useful online resource
www.craftgate.com

Hobby Lobby
Stores nationwide
www.hobbylobby.com

Jo-Ann Fabric and Craft Store
Stores nationwide
1–888–739–4120
www.joann.com

Michaels
Stores nationwide
1–800–642–4235
www.michaels.com

Paper Source
Stores nationwide
www.papersource.com

UK STOCKISTS

Cass Art
Stores across London
020 7619 2601
www.cassart.co.uk

Craft Creations
Online store
01992 781900
www.craftcreations.com

Crafty Devils
Online store
01271 326777
www.craftydevilspapercraft.co.uk

Etcetera
Vintage homewares
07977161915
etcetera-online.co.uk

Hobbycraft
Stores nationwide
0330 026 1400
www.hobbycraft.co.uk

John Lewis
Stores nationwide
03456 049 049
www.johnlewis.com

Paperchase
Stores nationwide
www.paperchase.co.uk

Shepherds Papers
London paper store
020 7233 9999
store.bookbinding.co.uk

INDEX

Note: **Bold** page numbers refer to templates

A

adhesives 10
alphabet
  garland 48–9, **129**
  magnets 111–13, **138**
ampersand shopper 56–9, **130**
appliqué
  stitches 110
  wall hanging 114–5, **139**

B

birthday cards 48
blackboard, letter-shaped 63–5, **131**

C

capital,
  concrete 94–5, **132**
  corrugated 82–5, **132**
cardboard see posterboard
card stock (card) 14–17, 34–5, 48–9, 68–
  70, 75, 82, 85, 88, 89, 91, 96, 102
coffee sack letters 92–3, **135**
comic capitals, 3-D 42–3, **127**
corrugated capital 82–5, **132**
cutouts
  industrial-style 102–3, **136**
  notebook 44–5, **127**
cutting 11

F

fabric 108, 111, 114
  magnets 111–13, **138**
fairground flair 68–71, **133**
fiberfill (stuffing) 111, 113
flags, paper 22, 36
flowers, paper 22
foamboard 84, 110
  lollipop letters 30–33, **136**
fruit-crate letter 80–81
fruit-crates 94

G

garland, alphabet 48–9, **129**
garlands 7, 36
gift 14, 26, 66, 118
gift tag 75
giftwrap 88

I

industrial-style cutouts 102–3, **136**
ink 66
  printing 72–5

J

jacket, studded 121–3, **140**

L

labels 18, 88
lampshade, punched 46–7, **128**
letter
  art, printed 72–5
  fruit-crate 80–81
  light-it-up 96–9, **136**
  nailed outline 100–101, **137**
  silver leaf 34–5, **124**
  vintage fabric 108–10, **139**
  weathered wood 78–9
  wire and paper 18–21, **137**
  wire cage 104–5, **137**
letters
  3-D
    comic capitals 42–3, **127**
    painted outline 60–62
  coffee sack 92–3, **135**
  colorful paper bead 22–5
  foamboard lollipop 30–33, **136**
  Mexican paper 36–8, **126**
  painted and printed wood 52–5, **130**
  slot-together 88–91, **135**
  string 86–7, **134**
  vintage graphic letters 14–17,
    34–5, **125**
letter-shaped blackboard 63–5, **131**
light-up letter 96–9, **136**
lollipop letters, foamboard 30–33, **136**

M

magazine pages 18, 88
magnets, mix-it-up fabric 111–13, **138**
materials 8
Mexican paper letters 36–8, **126**
mounting board 96, 98

N

nailed letter outline 100–101, **137**
newspaper 18, 56, 68, 102
notebook cutouts 44–5, **127**

O

outline, nailed 100–101, **137**
overlay, tissue paper 39–41

P

painted
  3-D outline 6062
  and printed wood letter 52–5, **130**
paper
  bags 88
  bead letters 22–5
  cartridge 26, 28, 29, 39, 41, 72
  handprinted 18
  patterned 48,
  photo-transfer 118
patterns 36, 66
personalized pebbles 66–7, **132**
photo transfer 118–20, **139**
pillow cover 114
planks 78
plywood 63–5
posterboard (cardboard) 14–17, 42, 43,
  48, 75, 82–5, 86, 87, 88, 89,
printed letter art 72–5
printers' letter blocks 7, 72
punched lampshade, simple 46–7, **128**

R

rubber stamps 72, 75

S

scoring 11
scrollwork, sculptural 26–9
shelf 53
shopper, ampersand 56–9, **130**
silver leaf letter 34–5, **124**
slot-together letters 88–9, **135**
stars, paper 22
stencils 56, 102
string letters 86–7, **134**
studded jacket 121–3, **140**
suppliers 141

T

tassels, paper 18
techniques 8
  cutting 11
  scoring 11
  scrollwork 26–9
  tracing 10
templates 124–140
  enlarging 9
tissue paper 33
  overlay 39–41
tools 8
tracing 10
transfer, photo 118–20, **139**
typefaces 6, 39, 48, 75, 111, 114
typography 6, 68

V

vintage fabric letter 108–10, **139**
vintage graphic letters 14–17,
    34–5, **125**
votive 46

W

wall hanging, appliqué 114–5, **139**
wallpaper 14, 30
weathered wood letter 78–9
wire and paper letter 18–21, **137**
wire cage letter 104–5, **137**
wood, letter, painted and printed 52–5,
    130

ACKNOWLEDGMENTS

Thanks so much to Cico for giving me the opportunity to do what I love best, designing and making. A special thanks to Cindy Richards, Sally Powell, Patricia Harrington, and Anna Galkina, who are always such a pleasure to work with and make everything run so smoothly. Thank you to Anna Southgate for such careful editing and to Claire for her beautiful photography. Thanks to Shelly and Shaun for the loan of their house, full of wonderful props. Thank you Milly, Florence, and Henrietta for all your creative feedback, and to Harvey for agreeing, (slightly reluctantly) to model the jacket for me. Finally, a special thanks to Ian who gave me the key to his tool shed!